SILENCED NO MORE

EMPOWERING THE NEXT GENERATION OF WOMEN

SANCTUARY PUBLISHING

CONTENTS

For all the women across all generations who felt like they needed to stay silent about their lived experiences, this one's for you!

Together we rise!

INTRODUCTION

You are invited to embark on an evolution of self through reading the stories held within this book. This collaborative, multi-author book —*Silenced No More: Empowering the Next Generation of Women* is here to show you eleven different perspectives from female leaders on what it means to them to no longer be silent. To no longer be silent about their power as women on this earth. To no longer be silent about their lived experiences that made them who they are today. To no longer be silent about the aspects of life that most want to sweep under the rug.

It is the act of remaining silent that robs us of our power. Most generational and societal norms have been rooted in staying silent about our traumas, being uneducated about our bodies, and remaining blind to our innate ability to go after our desires. Now is the time for women to hold strong and hold a mirror to each other about what you've felt deep within all along.

Indeed, we do have a say, we are powerful, and we are never alone in what we have been through. We have the ability to create the change that we desire to see take shape in the world. It all begins within us. Through reading these stories I invite you to explore. Where in your life have you kept silent?

May these stories mirror to you what you are truly capable of. By being, connecting, and sharing our stories, through our embodied power, change can be created. Not just for fellow women, but for future generations to come!

Standing in your truth is not about asking for validation; your truth is known within you. It is only to yourself that you need to no longer push away the pieces of you desiring to be heard. This is how we start evolving, through knowing that, as long as we have ourselves, we are capable of anything.

Through their courage in sharing their stories, my hope for you is that you are reminded that you are not alone and that you get to meet a new piece of yourself that ignites the way forward for your personal growth and transformation.

Annette Maria
Liberated Leadership Coach + Intuitive
Founder of Sanctuary Publishing

ANIKO FISCH

A RECLAMATION OF HEALTH

I watched my grandma fall apart while I was growing up. As a kid, I just thought she was old and it was what happened to all old people. Looking back, I realize she was only in her fifties (far too young) when her health deteriorated.

I can still smell the insulin. It radiated out of her pores every time she injected herself. I can still see the countless colorful pill containers piled on her coffee table. Occasionally, while my cousins and I were having pillow fights, we would notice her teeth in a glass of water on her nightstand. A haunting image that sticks with me to this day.

I used to have a blast zooming down the aisles of the grocery store on my grandma's four-wheeled walker. But before long, I had to give up this pastime, because she started needing her walker for even the smallest of movements. By this stage she already had a hip and knee replacement, a kidney and gallbladder removal, and a hysterectomy. She barely had any body parts to spare.

During my teen years, her health continued to deteriorate. My once jovial, lively grandmother was a shell of her former self. It was hard to miss the connection: the more pills she took, and the more hospital visits she had, the less vibrant she became, and the more junk food she ate to console herself. It seemed she had lost the willpower to get herself out of this cycle.

My grandma was a Hungarian immigrant to Canada. Her mother, a Siberian peasant, gave birth to her while plowing the fields in Hungary. My great grandmother gave birth to six babies in that field — but only two survived. After giving birth to my grandma, my great grandmother hid her newborn so that her masters wouldn't see and continued plowing as though nothing had happened. The blood of my maternal lineage carries the essence of a survivor—resourceful, resilient, and deeply connected to the land.

My grandma always knew what to do when it came to taking care of my health. She and my mother cured all my sniffles and aches with healing remedies: chicken soup, bone marrow, herbal teas, raw honey, garlic, and ginger. She had a green thumb; her pride and joy was her garden. She always made sure that the birds had plenty to eat, and that the butterflies and bees were happy with her flower selection. She was a plant and animal whisperer extraordinaire.

How could this survivor so connected to the wisdom of the land have become so disconnected from the wisdom of her own body? She cared for my health with remedies handed down from her ancestors, yet she lost all faith in her body's ability to receive the powers of these remedies for her own healing.

I witnessed my grandma die at the hands of Big Pharma, and I vowed to never go down the dangerous route of allopathy (unless, of course, I needed to get an arm sewn back on). I developed a serious mistrust of all things "medical."

My mother was also disillusioned by the medical paradigm, so she began to take me to acupuncturists and other more holistic practitioners while I was growing up. But, occasionally, she took me to the doctor to get an obligatory shot for school or to get antibiotics for an infection. Almost every time we went this route, my body mounted a wild, inflammatory reaction to the medical interventions.

The antibiotic-style approach of killing everything out of fear of hypothetical illness never made a lick of sense to me. When my parents and I moved from Europe to America I was ten, and I remember how strict some of my American friends' parents were about washing or sanitizing our hands every time we came indoors. Why are we killing something invisible to the eye? Surely these germs can't be that bad if we can't even see them, I thought to myself.

In my early twenties, I met a holistic doctor who became my mentor. He took me on a mind-blowing exploration into the worlds of German New Medicine, emotional healing, and the terrain approach to healing (which focuses on healing the body from the inside-out by harmonizing the inner terrain, rather than focusing on external factors such as germs and viruses). He taught me that germs are our helpers, that contagions don't exist in the way we think they do, and that the root cause of all illness is either an emotional or toxic imbalance, or sometimes a combination of both. I had finally found someone who confirmed my gut feelings about the nonsensical ways most of us viewed sickness and health. His proof was in his hundreds of happy, healthy patients, many of which had healed from supposedly incurable or terminal illnesses by natural, non-invasive means.

Now that I had confirmation, my indignation was fired up!

I dedicated the next few years of my life going deep down rabbit holes and questioning everything I'd been taught by the medical paradigm. Lab tests, mammograms, ultrasounds, x-rays, vaccines, and antibiotics...I found proof to debunk the necessity or safety of all of these, and I even drove myself a little crazy uncovering some of the more nefarious motives behind certain medical practices. Iatrogenesis (i.e, death by a doctor) is the third leading cause of death in the US. *Why wasn't this headline news???*

During this time, I started studying nutrition so I could help people take care of their health by using food as their primary medicine. After doing a couple of years of nutrition coaching, I discovered quantum physics and became fascinated by the science that proves what the ancients already knew for millennia—we are all made up of energy. I started to learn an array of energy healing methods to complement my health coaching.

I thought I had it all figured out. "Just stay away from the poisons of the system," I told my clients. "Eat organic, pesticide-free food, avoid environmental toxins, do some energy healing, and you'll be A-okay."

That's the way I was living my life, and it seemed to be working quite well for me. But one day my life flipped upside-down. I was at a wedding chatting with someone one moment, and the next moment my vision blacked out and I was sliding down to the floor. At first, I shrugged it off as a freak incident. Little did I know that this would be the start of a several-year-long journey into the depths of a mystifying, debilitating illness.

I was sure I was dying. A barrage of symptoms hit me like a sledgehammer practically overnight. Fatigue so draining that my legs felt like lead when I walked. Blurry vision to the point where I felt like I was looking at the world through dirty plexiglass. Dizziness and brain fog so intense that thinking became a herculean effort. My digestion was wildly unpredictable. My sensitivity to light and noise became maddening. The worst symptom was the panic attacks, which, occasionally, sent me to the hospital. After a couple of major attacks, the anxiety stuck around. The anticipation of these episodes left me constantly on edge, nervous about any subtle change in my environment, and scared of any person who tried to come up to talk to me. I was constantly on high alert, and then I would crash from the exhaustion of being on high alert. Repeat cycle.

These symptoms were so terrifying and uncontrollable that, at first, I even put my mistrust of medical doctors aside. Surely, something this serious must be addressed by the experts, I thought. But none of the doctors could figure out what was wrong. All my test results came back normal. "There's nothing we can do to help your condition," I was told.

Knowing that the allopathic route didn't have the answers, I gathered every last bit of energy I had left to find other ways to conquer whatever mysterious illness had taken over my body. I spent the majority of the next two years at dozens of holistic practitioners' offices. Nutrient drips, acupuncture, chelation therapy, hyperbaric oxygen, ozone therapy, Chinese medicine, energy healing, hypnosis, juice fasting, colonics—you name it, I tried it. Most of these treatments triggered massive detox reactions in my body. Some even sent me back to the hospital. I had the voices and differing opinions of countless practitioners swarming in my head at all times, and I was bending over backward to follow their protocols to perfection. My intuition had been entirely drowned out. I had no sense of what was truly helping me, or what was adding fuel to the fire.

By that point, I had two men in my life whose opinions I cared a lot about—my father and my boyfriend. These two men couldn't bear seeing me so unwell. They wanted me *fixed.* They were problem-solvers used to finding solutions and mending what was broken. So, my desire to be proactive about my situation was amplified even more by my desire to pacify their worries.

Yet, each passing month I felt worse. No matter what I tried, I kept spiraling down into what seemed like a bottomless pit. I had to stop working, and I spent most days in bed crying to a higher power for some relief.

One year into this health challenge, my boyfriend and I decided to move from California to Australia in hopes of finding better healing solutions as well as being closer to nature and his family. The stress of the move and the pressure I put on myself to get better became too much to handle. My health plummeted even further. After a year in Australia, my boyfriend told me that he could no longer hold space for what I was going through. We broke up and I flew to Canada, in shambles, to be with my mother.

I spent the first few weeks in Canada too devastated and unwell to do anything besides sleep, eat, sob in my mother's arms, and cuddle my dog. I allowed myself to just be because the thought of *doing* was too overwhelming. It was the first time in over two years that I allowed my body to relax and soften into the discomfort, simply because I had no more fight left. I let myself go, and I gave up.

And then, something miraculous happened. I started to heal.

My break-up and the resulting move back to North America were huge blessings in disguise. They forced me into a turning point and allowed me the space to see why the two years leading up to that point had been so fruitless. I had been running on a hamster wheel trying to mend what I perceived as a broken body. Why? Because most of us in the Western world have been conditioned to believe that symptoms are malfunctions within the body that need quick fixes much like a mechanic would repair a car.

For most of my life, I had been blaming the medical paradigm for bulldozing over mother nature, feminine-form, and intuitive healing arts with its rigid science. I was angry at the system for blinding my grandma to her healing abilities. I was enraged at the allopathic model for teaching us to not trust our bodies and even worse—teaching us to fear our faulty bodies. The speed it up, slow it down, cut it open, or numb it out approach to symptoms represented everything that I found so harmful about the system. Yet, during the first couple of years of illness, I was doing the same thing that I was accusing the Western medical model of doing: I was not trusting my body's innate healing wisdom. I was seeing this health challenge as something wrong, random, and uncontrollable that needed to be fixed by an external (albeit holistic) authority. I was rushing my healing process and perceiving my symptoms as horrors that needed to be swiftly eliminated. In short, I was trying to avoid discomfort at all costs.

When I started allowing the innate healing powers of my body to take the wheel, everything shifted. When I softened into trusting the wisdom of my body, my nervous system relaxed enough for healing to take place. When I stopped viewing practitioners as my saviors, but rather as my cheerleaders cheering on my body's amazing healing abilities, I started to enjoy the journey I was on.

Shortly after this turning point, I met a marvelous stranger who introduced me to a holistic health care system called BodyTalk. After one session I knew I had found the type of health care I was needing all along (and that I would eventually practice myself). It's a modality that works *with* the intelligence of the body rather than against it. It's an approach that allows the body's innate wisdom to lead you gently and intuitively to the root causes of imbalance. I went from having a big arsenal of different treatments and modalities to just receiving the occasional BodyTalk session. Aside from that, rest and connection with nature became my primary medicine.

Once I simplified and slowed down, I was able to create space for magic to unfold. As Lao Tzu said, "Nature does not hurry, yet everything is accomplished." There is a prevailing myth that complex health issues need a complex solution when, in truth, slowing down and simplifying are much more powerful remedies. Most of our modern-day illnesses stem from our rushed lives and our disconnection from our very nature. Our nature is nature. We have the incredible capacity to self-regulate and self-heal, but we must be able to slow down enough to notice when we are off balance. The body's gentle whispers for rest and restoration can only go on for so long before they start turning into unavoidable screams.

At this point on my journey, I chose to change my story. Instead of desperately asking, Why is this happening *to* me? I started asking the question, Why is this happening *for* me? This nuance was life changing. I went from perceiving my situation as a curse, to seeing it as one of the biggest blessings in my life that couldn't have happened any other way. This health challenge got me to exactly where I needed to be on my path and taught me more than my twenty five years of education ever could have.

This switch in perspective became an invitation for me to step out of victim consciousness. For years, I was accusing the medical system of turning their patients into scared victims who could only be saved by the gods in white coats. Yet I was keeping myself in victimhood by fully outsourcing my health to experts and trendy wellness fads, all while abandoning all trust within myself and my body. I was perpetuating the mentality that healing requires an external savior.

Most healthcare is focused on the war against disease: us versus our symptoms. Even the natural healing world is often steeped in the fearful language of victim versus perpetrator: "eat this to *combat* aging," "drink this to *shield* yourself from toxins," or "take this herb to *eliminate* that symptom," take this *anti*-viral supplement." Instead of fearing our alleged vulnerabilities, isn't it much more empowering to know our bodies are always striving to keep us in balance, to know that any symptoms we experience are signs from the body that realignment and healing are underway, and to know that we ought to slow down to support this self-regulating process? Isn't it exhilarating to know that nature does nothing in vain? I am reminded of a powerful quote from *The Gene Keys: Embracing Your Higher Purpose* by Richard Rudd that stresses the detriment of fear to our health: "All physical disease is rooted in the frequencies of fear. As humanity evolves beyond its current stage, it will eventually move beyond fear, which will result in the end of all disease."

If my grandma were still alive today, I would invite her to sit in her garden all day, marvel at her plants, breathe into her heart space, and stop waging war against her body. I would tell her that she has nothing to fear. I would let her know that she is powerful beyond her wildest imagination, and that she deserves the same loving care and nurturing that she so freely gives to her plants, animals and grandchildren. Most importantly, I would thank her for all that she went through in her life to inspire my journey to reclamation.

If you are looking for someone to support you on your healing journey, and if you are feeling inspired to learn new ways to tune into your body's inner wisdom and support your natural state of vibrant health, I would be honored to connect with you and be your healing guide.

ABOUT THE AUTHOR

ANIKO FISCH

Aniko started her journey in the health and healing world with her passion for food. After several years of studying and coaching nutrition, she realized that healthy eating is only a small part of lasting health. This realization brought her down a path of exploration into the world of quantum biology and energy medicine. After learning several methods of energy healing, life took an unexpected turn when she started to experience a mysterious illness that left her "out of commission" for several years. Through her journey back to health, she gained an entirely new perspective on why the body expresses imbalance through dis-ease. The insights she has gained and the tools and mindset she has developed have had the most profound effect on her own healing journey. They form the foundations of the work she does with clients. As a healing guide, Aniko supports her clients in reclaiming their health and their innate ability to thrive.

Learn more and connect here:

www.innerthrivewellness.com

aniko@innerthrivewellness.com

DOREEN M. LETOFSKY

PAPER GOWNS

I stood in the dusty library holding the hands of both my mother and father, a sudden streak of panic raced through me, and I squeezed. *He is here!* I thought. *He's here to take pictures and to take that step into the next chapter of our lives together.* We were mere hours away from wedded bliss filled with all the graces a Jewish wedding offered—the veiling of the bride, standing under the chuppah, the circling of the groom, the blessings to be bestowed upon us, and the breaking of glass. This was the first day of the rest of our lives. The day that I magically, by virtue of the impending ceremony, had gained the right to pursue my grandest dream—becoming a mother.

As a child, when we would play "house," I always wanted to be the "mom," and usually I was. This was my favorite role. I would be the one to take care of and love on the "kids" during these make-believe games. Whenever I had the chance in real life, I would be the first one to ask to hold or feed any of the babies we knew or to take the younger kids outside to play or organize games inside for them. I would often hear praises like, "you are such a great little mom," or "you are going to be such a great mom one day."

Fast forward to 1999, I was married, and I was so ready to expand my family that I was having "mommy and me" dreams. In the dream, I was at a baby gym, and I was encouraging my baby boy to reach beyond his accomplishments so far and I asked him to come to me on the other side of the mat. He was so little, but he was watching me, and he was moving all his limbs, almost as if he was swimming on the mat. He had not moved from his belly. I crawled to him and told him he was doing great, and he's such a big boy as I picked him up and nuzzled his neck. He squealed and let out a big belly laugh that melted my insides completely. I simply could not help myself and I kissed all over his sweet little baby body, and he squealed even more.

When I would wake, I would be painfully reminded I was not a mother. Not yet. I prayed silently. Or maybe it was more like I begged. *Why was it not yet my time to be a mother? Was my day still coming?*

During my waking hours, I was busy stocking prenatal supplies: basal body temperature thermometers, a calendar, ovulation test kits, and pregnancy tests all neatly gathered in the nightstand drawer on my side of the bed. On top of the nightstand were books about how the female reproductive system works, about balancing hormones, and about preparing for a baby. Additionally, I was desperately trying to make the task of trying to conceive not become a checklist item or one more 'have to'. It was enough that I needed to be ready even if I was not ready, so the least I could do was make those moments as spontaneous as possible and be one hundred percent "in the mood." This was not easy when sex was about getting pregnant, and you had a twelve-hour window to get it done. After all, we both had jobs and did not need sex to become a job too.

Initially, I had not been counting. I had documented everything on the calendar though. Every ever-so-faint positive test result I had would then, within 48 hours, turn into "Period Day 1." Every. Single. Time. *What the fuck? What was going on here?* I thought to myself.

I continued to research, read, and then re-read. Thoughts swirled in my head, *what am I missing? I am getting pregnant, but I am not staying pregnant. Something is not right. What am I missing?*

I had prepared my body to be ready to grow a baby since saying yes to marriage almost two years before finding myself in the middle of the most emotionally devastating journey I never imagined taking.

I stopped drinking coffee and alcohol; I started taking prenatal vitamins; I used natural progesterone cream on my abdomen. But the most spectacular thing I did was tune into my body. I paid such close attention to what my body was doing daily that I knew exactly when I was ovulating and from which ovary.

We are well into 2000 now and when I looked at my tracking calendar on one typical summer day, I realized I was seven days past my period start date. I inhaled. I exhaled. *Doreen do not celebrate yet,* I thought. *We have been here before. This time will be different. Seriously, it has to be different! I cannot be the only woman in this family to not have a baby, right? I mean, everyone else has been successfully pregnant and mostly did not even try to be. Take the test. Take the test. G-d and you are in this together. Take the test. Then celebrate.* I took the test. And there was that faint pink line—again. It was faint but not as faint as before. *Well, it looks stronger. This month you are a mother-to-be.*

Then I silently prayed, "G-d, I know you know this is the only thing I have ever wanted this badly, please stay with me and let this be my time. I have suffered enough loss. Please give me this baby." I then said it aloud. *Doreen get it together now; you have to go to your in-laws tonight.*

While we sat around the dining room table, after finishing dinner, with all my husband's family, I excused myself to go to the bathroom. I sat down on the toilet and checked in with my body, I felt the cramps starting and saw spots of red on my panty liner. I wiped—damn it! *Not again. Not. Again.* I could not stop the tears. *When was this going to stop? What the hell was I being punished for? Who did I piss off? Why does no one want me to be his or her mommy? What the fuck?*

"Doreen get it together!" I scolded myself for the second time in as few hours. I went down the steps, and I saw that my brother-in-law, sister-in-law, and father-in-law had moved to the living room. I walked past them, avoiding eye contact with everyone except my husband. He was still in the dining room speaking with his mother. I walked directly to him and barely uttered, "Can I have the car keys please?" He gave me a questioning look and all I said was, "Period." Then I heard my very well-intended, but often misguided mother-in-law bellow, "Doreen, What's the matter?" in that (you know if you know) Jewish mother voice. My husband shot her a look that I read as "Just stop!"

I drove the mile to CVS, bought tampons and pantyliners, and then drove back to my in-law's house. I was still unable to control the overwhelming sadness and the tears that kept coming. I inhaled. I exhaled. I told myself to keep breathing. When I walked into the house, everyone stopped talking and no one looked at me. The air was thick and uncomfortable. I imagine no one knew what to say to me at that moment. That moment that should have been private and all mine, but it was at the forefront of that evening's summer barbeque. We left after this because the awkwardness was simply too much.

A few months later, I checked the calendar again and realized, as I counted, I was five...six... seven days late. Again. I inhaled. I exhaled. I took a test. There it was! Finally! That pink line was the most vibrant yet! I crossed my fingers and prayed silently, *please G-d. Please.* I would wrap the test the next day and give it to my husband to share the news. The next day came, and I chickened out. I waited another day. I took another test. Yes! The pink line was still there! FINALLY! I wrapped the test and gave it to my husband. He opened it, smiled, looked at me, and said, "Really?" I repeated back to him, "Really!"

After the first positive, I was counting days. Seven. Seven days, one week. I had made it a whole week past the first test. *Phew,* I thought. *I can make plans this time! Someone wants to call me mommy.* I had counted the weeks to forty. This baby would be due in early July. Perfect! I would not be pregnant all summer. I would have a summer baby. I was so excited for this. *This is why they say pregnant women glow,* I thought as I felt the energy of the initial excitement bubbling from me. I wondered if I would give myself away or if I would be able to contain myself and wait to share this news until I was further along? *I would probably give myself away, I deduced.* I did not hide emotions well after all so it must have been written all over my face.

About thirty minutes after an intense conversation in my head about pregnant women glowing, I felt a pang in my gut. *Wait, that feels like a cramp. No. No. No. Not again. Not this time. NO! NO! NO! NO! I do not understand why this happening again.* The tears began to flow. I was at work. I convinced myself that I just needed to keep working. I needed this day to just be normal. I had a later appointment with my chiropractor who knew I was pregnant and would know I was losing this baby too. This was the eighth time. The eighth miscarriage. *Maybe if I pretended that day was normal then it would be normal and this nightmare would go away.*

Later as I sat in the exam room at the chiropractor's office the doctor asked me if I was okay and I told him I had to be okay. I needed that day to be normal. He said, "But today is not normal." No, today had not been normal. *I still am not going to be a mother, I thought.*

We had been on this journey for over a year. I had a collection of positive pregnancy tests and no babies to show for them. I felt like I was spinning. I had no idea how to move past this insanity. I did not know if I was ever going to be a mom. I did not know how to get off this rollercoaster. My obstetrician told me he thought it was time to refer me to a fertility specialist. So I went to see the new doctor looking for answers. Hoping for answers and scared of what those answers would be.

The next year was all about more of the same—trying, tracking, faint pink lines, and miscarrying. Six more times. The next year was also filled with testing: tests for me and tests for my husband. There were sperm counts, blockage tests, blood tests. The only difference between my tests and my husband's test were the stirrups. I must have clocked more hours hanging out in stirrups and paper gowns, in one year, than the average woman will in a lifetime. I was at the fertility specialist two to four times a month and at each appointment, she did an internal ultrasound.

Do you know how an internal ultrasound is performed? The doctor has a wand that she inserts into your vagina. They roll it around to look at your ovaries and take pictures of the follicles (early eggs), as they form, to understand your cycle. The bottom line of all the tests? Everything appeared to be "normal" and in "working order." *Wait? What? How was this normal? How does one person over the course of two years have fourteen pregnancies and still, no one was calling me mama?*

"Doreen, this leaves us with how to get you pregnant now and keep you pregnant. We have tools to use to get you there. And I will be monitoring you every step of the way. How does this sound," the doctor asked. *How does this sound? This sounds scary as hell and like more heartache!* Aloud, I said, "Sounds like a plan! What is the next step?"

Clomid was the next step. I took Clomid once, in November 2001. We continued the internal ultrasounds, monitored my blood weekly while we watched for those follicles to form, so we would know exactly when I was ovulating. She said to keep doing everything the way we had been initially. Ultimately, we were to stop having sex. It sounds counter intuitive, right? We would be scheduled to be artificially inseminated once they could predict ovulation. The process involved collecting the semen sample at home in a sterile container, then put it in a sock, and place that sock in between my breasts under my sweater. (This is the warmest place on a woman's body.) Next, drive it to the doctor's office within one hour, for the health of the sperm. Once at the doctor's office, the technician takes the sample, removes the sperm from the semen, and "washes" it. Finally, they put the sperm in synthetic semen inside a plastic syringe and insert it into my cervix, so that the sperm can be injected as close to the released egg as possible while I hung out, in stirrups, for an hour lying on a wedged pillow. I did this twice—December 2, 2001, and December 4, 2001.

On December 10, 2001, I was attending a meditation circle, and, for me, the meditation seemed to go on longer than I needed it to. I opened my eyes and looked around the room. When I looked to my left, I saw my recently deceased aunt walking toward me. I watched her and wondered what she was doing there. She told me that I was getting what I wanted. I knew at that moment I was, in fact, pregnant. I did a little happy dance in my seat and chanted to myself, "I am pregnant. I am pregnant." This was still very scary, but I felt those words were meant to assure me that this time was different. This time I will hold on to this baby.

The blood test on December 17, 2001, confirmed I was pregnant, and both my HCG (the pregnancy growth hormone) levels and progesterone levels were in great ranges. The blood test on December 24, 2001, however, showed that my progesterone levels had dropped so low that I was in danger of miscarrying. Again. *No! Not again! How do we fix this? I cannot lose another baby!* I pleaded to myself. The doctor told me she would put me on progesterone suppositories and, by three in the afternoon, I had started using them. Answered prayers.

On August 28, 2002, my rainbow baby was born. Lindsey Skyler–my little big bird. Perfect. Tiny. Ten fingers and ten toes. The first person to call me mommy. My baby that took three years in the making. She was so hard-to-create, yet so easy-to-raise.

I did conceive another baby in January 2004. The day I realized that I had missed my period I went into a full-on panic. Now I knew that I did not produce enough progesterone, so I had a real chance of losing this baby if I did not act fast. I called the fertility specialist that day and she ran a blood test and got me started on progesterone suppositories immediately.

On October 1, 2004, my second baby was born. Jaime Alexandra—my fairy child. She loves the earth and needs to move her big muscles even to this day. She was my easy-to-grow, and hard-to-raise baby. She, also, is my last child.

I originally wanted four children. I wanted boys and girls. In spite of this I am still one of the lucky ones. Some women never succeed at becoming a mother and I did. I went through hell to get to the other side of the process. I have carried the pain and shame of fourteen failed pregnancies. I have been told many things through the process. I was told that "I should be over it by now," "It's not as bad as having a stillborn," "You are ok with your friend's baby, why are you upset that your sister-in-law is pregnant?" and my favorite, "What the hell are you waiting for? You should be popping out babies by now!"

If I could leave you with one thought, please remember that everyone's journey is theirs and very personal. Please keep your ideas and thoughts in check, because more women than we realize experience infertility in one form or another. The loss of a pregnancy is a miscarriage whether that loss occurs at five days, five weeks, or five months and this kind of loss is worthy of their grief. For as long as they need to grieve. No one gets to shame them for grieving or feeling sad. Also, they get to ask for help. Do not wait an entire year if you know something is wrong, be your own advocate. And doctors are scientists. Scientists need to have a term or process for everything. The term "chemical pregnancy" is just a term. If you have a sperm and an egg come together, that is a baby no matter how short it exists. If you lose that pregnancy, you have lost a baby. Period.

ABOUT THE AUTHOR

DOREEN M. LETOFSKY

Doreen M. Letofsky is an accountant specializing in the details and she has been working in this field for over thirty years. Doreen has worked in public accounting as well as the private sector including non-profits. She has a bachelor of science in accounting from the former Beaver College, now known as Arcadia University, she has passed the CPA exam, and she keeps current on all tax law changes and anything critical to her business. Doreen has a passion for learning and has been nurturing her intuitive side as well as learning American Sign Language (ASL) which has been a lifelong interest. Recently, Doreen became a published author and is very excited to continue her writing career. Additionally, Doreen is a single mom of two teenage girls and shares her home with her dog and guinea pig.

Doreen is also enjoying sharing her life with Charles, with whom she has discovered a love for sporting clays and travel.

Learn more and connect here:

www.linkedin.com/in/doreen-m-letofsky-accountant

BkkgByDML@gmail.com

JANET LYNN FILER

RAISING HOPE

"The child who is not embraced by the village will burn it down to feel its warmth"- African Proverb

I moved us for peace and safety. I never expected a war to come from within Kelly, my first son.*

The sound of handcuffs clicking around Kelly's thin wrists echoed inside my head. I wasn't sure which was louder, my heartbeat or those clicks. The police officers' voices were distorted like a record played on the wrong speed. I knew I was there inside our house. I saw myself standing by the French doors, but I was not truly present. My fear left no room for me to fit inside the same person.

The red and blue lights strobed brightly, pushing through the gaps in the living room blinds. They sliced every surface in the room. I could not look away even though they stung my eyes. I don't think I even blinked.

A police officer took Kelly into the cold November night air without a coat. I don't know if my son was wearing shoes, probably not. His anger kept him warm at least for a moment.

Breathe, I thought. Like so many other times, I had to tell myself to breathe. Was Kelly able to breathe?

I am assaulted, again, as images of my son and I replayed in my mind, forcing themselves to be seen and heard. A police officer asked me questions that weren't yet familiar. I answered them, because that's what I did, I complied. I know I accepted a pen and wrote our first story "on the record," because I'm looking at it now, all these years later.

My shoulder throbbed, yet I needed to check on the other boys.

I wondered what waking up the next morning–Thanksgiving morning–in juvenile detention felt like for Kelly. He was arraigned early that holiday morning, apparently free to go home. He was arrested for assaulting me, and barely twelve hours later, the officer supervising his pod called to let me know I needed to pick him up. Really? I was supposed to drive my son home this soon? I was in shock and not ready. I was grateful that compassionate officer heard the fear and bewilderment in my voice and gave me the gift of time when he said, "I'll let your son know things take longer to process on a holiday. We will see you tomorrow." He probably knew Kelly and I were going to see him again soon.

Real moms don't feel this kind of despair, I thought.

* * *

DEAR CHILD OF MINE,

You were born on your due date. After you were born, it took a few weeks to see this was not the right time or planet for you. Your dad called you Mount Vesuvius, after one of the most devastating volcanoes in the world. For years, I protested the comparison. Your whole life, I fought fiercely to protect you from this world.

I never expected to fight just as fiercely to protect myself from you.

You had your first seizure when you were a toddler. Even though my medical training told me what to do, my mom heart was terrified. You were limp, blue, and non-responsive in my arms. Minutes passed in slow motion, and it felt like years. It took the Paramedics more than ten minutes to arrive.

Also during your toddlerhood, you were diagnosed with a sensory processing disorder (a condition often associated with autism), and soon after you were expelled from childcare for "aggressive behavior." This sensory-seeking behavior landed you an Asperger's diagnosis before kindergarten.

I wish I could say your neurological differences explained everything that happened next, but we both know that wasn't entirely true.

As frightening and violent as many of your behaviors became, you still had an innocent tenderness that made you very vulnerable. Your tiny, little spirit chose me for a reason. I wish I knew what that reason was. I wish I could say you chose the right mom and flourished. Heck, I wish I could simply say you smiled often or slept well, but your fragile nervous system was not at peace. If only someone wiser and healthier could have told us what the future held and what we each needed to do.

Tiny little boy, I love you more each day,

Mom

* * *

I KNEW something was wrong when I turned on my bedroom light. Kelly said he didn't do it, that while he was in the shower, his friend stole all those things. In my anger, I couldn't believe him. I searched pawn shops trying to find our most sentimental pieces—especially the Celtic crosses given to my boys when their great-grandmother died and the Saint Raphael necklace I bought when I became a nurse. But nothing taken that day found its way back to us.

After the theft, a police officer recommended that I sleep with my keys and wallet in my pillowcase at night.

* * *

DEAR CHILD OF MINE,

You didn't know how to stop. Your inner motor was in constant motion.

When you were three years old, I took the training wheels off your tiny mountain bike, and you rode nonstop for seven miles. You would have ridden farther, but we ran out of trail.

When you were six, I took you and Ryan, your newborn brother, to my favorite beach in New Jersey. I wanted to show you the wild beach at the end of the island, one of the few happy places from my childhood. Sadly, I didn't know climate change and erosion had closed it to the public. The midday sand was excruciatingly hot on your bare feet. So that you could cool them in the ocean, I told you to run to the lifeguard stand and wait for me. You ran toward the lifeguards, but then you turned and sprinted up the shoreline. I shouted your name, but my voice was lost in the wind and the waves. I couldn't reach you. With pure fright, I watched you disappear over that first jetty.

I immediately reported you missing. The lifeguards used their whistles and radios, sounding an alarm up the island, but you had already outrun them. You ran for miles—over an hour—before a lifeguard spotted you. Matching your pace, the lifeguard jogged beside you. He called you by your name and asked you where your mom was. Still running, you turned toward him. Then you looked over your shoulder. Your face flushed with sudden fear. I wasn't running alongside you.

When you were seven, you asked for a skateboard. Not knowing better, we bought a one-by-six piece of wood and cut a rudimentary shape resembling the Penny Skateboards of the seventies. We repurposed the trucks and wheels from a cheap board from a toy store, added a little grip tape, and watched you soar! Your movements were magical and flawless. You dropped in on the vert ramps with perfect agility, grace, and talent. Your fluidity, courage, and persistence impressed the skate park staff, especially since you were riding the ergonomically inappropriate (and dangerous) board we had put together. We had you fitted for an authentic skateboard, and you were quickly invited to join the Ankle Biters, the youth skate team. On your own, you found a place where you belonged.

Just a few years later, you tried out for the Dew Tour and earned a premier spot on their Youth Demo Team. For the next two years, you skated vert ramps and freestyle courses all around the US and Canada with your childhood idols and heroes. You took that homemade board with you, turning it into a trophy collecting signatures of all the famous skaters you met: Bob Burnquist, Tony Hawk, Shaun White, Andy Macdonald and many others. You and I were so proud and excited!

I love you more each day,
Mom

* * *

THERE ARE moments when Kelly's childhood plays through my mind in vivid detail like a high-definition video. There are other times when it flickers and skips, like an old reel-to-reel movie. His addictions started when he was only thirteen years old. I will probably never know how many really terrible things happened because he was intoxicated.

It was a tremendous battle to protect Kelly, his little brother Ryan, and me. Tragically, it was impossible to protect all three at the same time.

I wasn't sure what I smelled that evening, but it was alarming and frightening. I sprinted up the stairs and pushed open Kelly's door. My eyes shot around his bedroom. I saw the fire: I saw him. His eyes were vacant and angry. His jaw was clenched. I had no idea what he was thinking, but the fire and his expression terrified me. I looked for something to extinguish the flames, but there was no water and nothing safe to smother them with. It did not make any sense for me to grab a book to cover the fire, but there was nothing else nearby. His charred furniture and the scorch marks scarring the bedroom door where a poster once had eyes proved there were more fires. If Kelly were going to burn down the house, Ryan needed a chance to escape, so I switched their bedrooms, moving Ryan to the top of the stairs and Kelly to the end of the hall. Although, after the fires, Ryan stopped sleeping upstairs altogether.

* * *

Dear child of mine,

Fire is a serious metaphor for you. You have a lot of energy and even more anger to burn, more anger than any child should ever have inside. Your first fire was terrifying; your last fire was pivotal.

When I opened our "Police Reports" folder, a pile of business cards with officers' names and our handwritten case numbers spilled into my lap. I am curious how many of these "events" you remember—shoving, choking, stealing, destroying things, putting holes in the walls. Which ones happened when you were high or drunk? You rarely smelled like alcohol, although there were mornings I couldn't wake you, nights you didn't come home. When you finally would come home, your shirt was sometimes stained with vomited blood. I worried about you greatly, but there were times I felt relieved you didn't come home, which doesn't feel like something I should tell you as your mom.

For years, I'm not sure which one of us hated the other more. I do know underneath all our contempt, darkness, and terror that I still loved you. In my pain and fear, I thought when you turned eighteen, I would walk away to let you self-destruct or survive on your own, but I couldn't do it.

Was addiction your way of self-medicating to fit inside the life you were given?

I have struggled to figure out what you and I could have done differently to change our story.

I work so hard to love you more each day,

Mom

* * *

Overtime, the judge's voice carried compassion and kindness for Kelly that I couldn't feel anymore. Kelly and I had exhausted every restorative program available in our county. The system moved our cases from criminal to civil court. Kelly went through diversion, mandated counseling, anger management classes, and chemical dependency programs. He had been ordered to take medications, but none of this was enforceable. As the judge spoke to Kelly that morning, he offered what he thought was an olive branch, but the words "house arrest," "ankle monitor," and "for two weeks" took my breath away. I thought I was going to collapse in the courtroom. My whole body shook uncontrollably. The victim's advocate held onto me to keep me upright. I pressed my hands into the railing in front of me, but they bounced off it from my adrenaline. My tears poured. I inhaled panic with each shallow breath. I told the judge that I heard him say that Kelly had rights, but I needed to know why his rights were more important than his younger brother Ryan's need for safety in our own home. I implored the judge to make a different decision. Ordering Kelly to stay home full-time with us was not going to end well.

My terror was raw and deep. How could the judge think that the safest place for the three of us was to be home together?

Within days, Kelly snapped. His rage had become quite dangerous. Call it frustration, boredom, impulsivity, or addiction, but what happened next unraveled our family. When the officers arrived that time, Ryan was still red and gasping for air. Kelly was never big, but he was incredibly strong. By then, the officers knew our address and names all too well. There was hardly a formality as they handcuffed Kelly and moved him out the front door. This time the charges were escalated to an assault in the second degree. Finally, the system was just as concerned for Ryan's safety as I was.

Kelly and I were in front of this judge over a dozen times already that year, and it was only the spring.

* * *

DEAR CHILD OF MINE,

In your teenage years, I learned that a mom could not get a restraining order against her child. I learned a mom could not surrender her child to foster care, even if she offered to pay child support. In a horribly broken system, I would be asked to choose which child I was willing to protect, and I would be judged many times for my answer to this no-win question.

I felt isolated and alone. I know you did too. It has been so painful to love you, but I still do.

The song I wrote for you during my pregnancy with you is playing in my head right now. Do you remember all the words? Can you hear my voice singing them?

"...Will I always hold you close...? ...Will you always have me near...?"

I am deeply sorry,

Mom

* * *

WHEN KELLY TURNED EIGHTEEN, he briefly moved into a friend's apartment, but a fight between them left him homeless. Kelly slept on benches during the day and stayed awake and alert overnight. To get out of the rain, he walked up and down the aisles at Walmart all night long. I didn't have the option to sleep during the day, and I didn't sleep well at night. Worry and fear for him overwhelmed me.

During this time, Kelly got a Taser to keep himself safe, a weapon he later threatened me with. At that moment, I couldn't think clearly, but my body knew what to do. It was as if I were being guided by a warrior or survivor archetype. I lifted my foot from the gas pedal. If I were going to be paralyzed on the highway, the last thing I needed was to accelerate the car.

My son terrified me at my core, but still, I fought for him.

* * *

DEAR CHILD OF MINE,

Did you know for years I imagined losing you, being told you died any number of tragic ways? I did this to prepare for what I thought was imminent grief. My mom heart was unspeakably torn and scarred. I did not think we would survive.

Your last arrest was traumatizing. You woke up, alone, in the county jail, real "adult jail," confused and afraid. You didn't know what had happened or why you were there.

The first time I visited, you told me about a kind, older inmate who was looking out for you. *What an interesting place to find a mentor,* I thought. When you told me this inmate reminded you of your PopPop, your worried eyes locked onto mine. I couldn't reach or comfort you through the thick glass in the visitor booth. The same weighted thought raced through both our minds, but neither of us spoke it aloud. Your PopPop (my father) died while incarcerated, weeks before your first arrest. You were now imprisoned with career criminals, men who'd spent their lives in the system. Many of these men had been imprisoned for decades. You knew you did not belong there.

This time, you and I both fought for you with an undeniable force of energy, will, and determination. You wanted a new life. We were going to change our story.

I couldn't afford the $250,000 bail that had been assessed, which meant you had to stay in the county jail. However, every day you woke up in that cell, your mind and body detoxed further. I borrowed money from my retirement account to hire your attorney, again. Weeks later, you were technically still incarcerated, but you were released into my custody to transport you to an inpatient rehab across the state. We both knew from your experiences as a teen that rehab programs definitely varied in quality. If you were going to get well, heal, and thrive you needed more than the twenty-one-day program I was driving you to.

I went online and printed an alphabetical list of every rehab in our state. I started calling each one asking if they offered a ninety-day inpatient program—none did. Somewhere in the letter "E" stack, a woman gave me the lead we needed. It turned out to be the name of a phenomenal out-of-state program. The next month, while you were still technically incarcerated, I flew you to California and you committed to the hard work. For the next eight months, you found your way to wholeness, and I was delighted to finally meet you, my first son.

With every year that passes, I am more impressed with the genuine courage and beauty inside you. You found the place where you belong and became the wonderful man you were meant to be.

Thank you for making me your mom.

I truthfully love you more each day,

Mom

* * *

I WANT to return to Kelly's childhood to give us a hint how our story ends.

I need to tell that mother who felt such profound despair, loss, resentment, alienation, and guilt that she has the strength to raise this boy and that he has the strength to not only stay alive, but to flourish. I need to tell that mother to trust and believe in herself and her son.

I need to let us know that we will both survive this journey.

Hearing these words would have been so powerful.

**All names have been changed to protect the individuals mentioned.*

ABOUT THE AUTHOR

JANET LYNN FILER

Janet Lynn Filer has dedicated her career to helping and healing children. She is a pediatric registered nurse and teacher with a bachelor's degree in psychology, a master's degree in early childhood special education, and an associate's degree in nursing. She has positively influenced the lives of hundreds of children and their families on their personal journeys through illnesses, injuries, cancer, developmental challenges, and mental health crises. She is a strong advocate for children with disabilities and an outdoor enthusiast. Her passion for adventure, hiking, and rock climbing relocated her from the East Coast to the Pacific Northwest where she has raised her two sons.

Although this is Janet's first published work, she has been writing for years and has many stories to share.

Learn more and connect here:
nursejanet456@gmail.com

JESSICA VERRILL

DEPROGRAMMING THROUGH AWARENESS

"That's not very ladylike!"

Insert eye roll. "GOOD!" I replied, "I don't want to be ladylike!"

I was in sixth grade home economics class and I had developed a nervous habit of biting my nails. I sat toward the back of the room while my teeth were chomping away on my already too-short manicure when my teacher paused her narrative to reprimand me.

Growing up female in a patriarchy there were spoken and unspoken rules. I came here to question and break the systems like many of the women in this book and readers seeing these words. I have never been one to accept things as they were or to allow myself to be irreparably broken. I push the line.

How often are we subject to bullshit?

You're much prettier when you smile.

Be a good girl.

Girls aren't good at math or science.

A woman's place is in the home.

Does your husband/boyfriend/partner let you do (insert activity)?

Are you on your period? Is that why you're so upset?

It's so great your husband babysits for you.

You're so sensitive/angry/upset/crazy/bitchy/insert whatever adjective needed for not conforming or having your own opinions.

Can't you take a joke? (Usually, after some misogynist or abusive remark is made.)

You're so bossy.

You're pretty/smart/good at technology/good at business/etc. for a woman.

You're never happy.

What others did I miss? I'm sure we could sit down for hours and still have more to share. As you're reading, assume there are many, many eye rolls happening as I recount the absurd ways growing up and living with anything other than a penis made me, and other women, subject to such bullshit.

The truth is, besides my natural rebellious spirit coming into play, I had watched the women around me wither away by being ladylike. It infuriated me to no end to see my mother's live-in boyfriend (who I often call my stepfather though they never married) finish dinner and immediately get up, move to the worn-in living room recliner, and flick on the TV to catch "60 Minutes" while we were left cleaning up. What gave him the right? Why did he think he was so special? And why did my mother allow it?

My maternal grandmother had it worse. My grandfather was an Italian with an angry temper, a liking for horse racing, and the old-school attitude of being able to hit your woman. Although, to me, he was kind and loving. He used to sing to me in Italian and give me huge hugs. I vividly recall a day when I was left with him while sick and, though partially paralyzed from numerous strokes, he managed to get to the kitchen to make me a pizza for lunch. The cheese went on first and then the tomato sauce. I assumed it was due to the damage in his brain, but it was one of the kindest moments and gestures. When he saw me, he would light up, and I would run to give him a big hug. A moment later, he would be screaming at my grandmother, cursing her up and down about something she did or did not do to his liking, and his language was so slurred that you could only occasionally make out the frequent f*ck you. Yet still, she cared for him, waited on him hand and foot, brought him to therapy, and loved him with a patience that rivaled any saint.

The Patriarchy.

They were all playing out their well-defined roles.

I'm not against roles. If you're reading this, and traditional gender roles feel perfectly aligned to your situation and it works, like really deep-down works—for everyone—then that is what matters. In my own home, my husband had traditionally provided the bulk of the family's finances, while I cared for my daughter and worked my business around his schedule. Not because I had to, but because I wanted to. Being a mother and staying with my daughter was a necessity for me. I personally could not drop her off at daycare every day for someone else to spend the days with her, so I created a life that centered around being a mother and this is continually my center point. Not because I needed to or was told I needed to, but because I see my role as a mother as sacred.

It's the choice, the awareness, and the consciousness that matters.

The truth is on some level, we learn how to play the game. For years, I worked in restaurants, mostly as a bartender. I was very good at my job and still, there were many times in my twenties when I played dumb and acted like I didn't know something. Otherwise, I would be subject to some old man mansplaining. Sometimes they'd be triggered by my intelligence or triggered by my being good at something other than pleasing a man and bearing children. Behind it all, I was playing their game, outsmarting them, taking their money, and luring them into giving me bigger tips through whatever persona I could intuitively sense they would respond best to.

Women learn to be aware of our surroundings at all times, to park close to the door, and be hyper-vigilant. At least, those of us with trauma at the hands of men do. One evening my husband drove the three of us to Target and, being Maine in the winter, it was already dark. As we pulled into the parking lot, illuminated by artificial lighting, he found a space that was away from the others, to avoid having his door being struck by the carelessness of others. I was shocked that he would consider parking so far away from the main entrance in an area that wasn't as brightly lit. I realized, he's never had to worry about the things I have, as a woman: he doesn't worry about being attacked, raped, or mugged (most likely by a man). He was free, in his mind, and was able to choose a parking spot based on what he wanted, and not what he needed for safety.

This is, partially, because he has only lived in Maine, an overall safe and quiet place, but mostly because he was born a different gender than I was and he is housed in a strong and masculine body. Physical fights were not out of the norm for him in his younger years and he never shows fear toward the thought of such altercations—something that undoubtedly attracted me to him. Safety. Protection.

I noticed something similar in my massage therapy business. Working primarily in the evenings after my daughter was born to switch off childcare with my husband, it was often dark outside when I finished and walked to my car. Female clients would almost always wait for me or at least ask to wait to make sure I was safe getting to my car. My male clients, whom I know respected and appreciated me, would leave without a second thought. Did they not care? Of course, not, some of them I had worked with weekly or monthly for over a decade. I knew about their work, their families, their hobbies, and their passions. They knew similar things about me as well, but it simply was not on their radar to be concerned with a dimly lit parking lot after dark.

I spent years working through trauma and triggers after multiple incidents of sexual assault and rape through my adolescence and young adulthood and also because of the relationships full of control, manipulation, and gaslighting. I wish I could say I was the exception, but unfortunately, most women I know have experienced abuse at the hands of men. Many are left wounded, angry, and fighting against anything with a penis while their nervous system goes haywire. Many cope by gaslighting themselves, brushing things off, pretending they didn't happen, or saying they didn't mean anything.

For me, I forged a path of calling out the objectification of women; educating others on the dark reality of pornography and the pornography industry as a whole (a majority of people in pornographic movies, and working as escorts, are human trafficking victims used for our entertainment or pleasure); and eventually as a soon-to-be mother, researching child sexual abuse, pedophilia, and refusing to turn a blind eye to any of it. Unless it happened to me. There's something that happens to you when you have been continuously objectified, used and abused over and over in your lifetime. You become desensitized to it. It becomes easier to pretend it didn't happen than to add it to the list of traumatic experiences that need to be healed.

Working in the service industry, both in restaurants and as a massage therapist, you learn how to de-escalate situations, how to avoid infuriating men, and how to avoid backlash for speaking up for yourself. But these aren't unique skills from these industries, they are things most women learn sooner or later, how to toe the fine line, how to keep yourself safe and not be subjected to the anger of a rejected man—a man that has often been conditioned his entire life to be entitled to what he wants, typically with little repercussion or backlash. What if you dared to be the one to stand up for yourself? I had already learned in so many ways that standing out meant that you would be attacked.

I don't need to get into the statistics, there are so many resources you can use to find these, but I am curious as to how many times you have found yourself minimizing an experience, making excuses for unacceptable behavior, or altogether ignoring it. Serving alcohol and being in social situations around alcohol, I found myself doing this a lot. Someone would make a sexually crude comment about you and you'd ignore him because he's drunk. Someone grabbed your ass and, as you pushed him away, he began to call you uptight, a prude, or insisted it was a harmless joke. Harmless for who? Certainly not you. While you tried to brush it off and get back to your conversation, your guard went up, you were violated—first physically and then emotionally by both him and you—and your energetic vibration went from one of joy or happiness to guilt and shame. In what alternative, messed-up reality do we live in where someone who is violated on so many levels is inflicted with loads of shame and guilt?

Energetically, shame and guilt are the two lowest vibrations and when we are in them it can feel impossible to move through. In this place, we aren't able to create a life we enjoy, and we tend to attract more instances of pain, trauma, or experiences of harmful energetic attachments to us, all of which further limit our experience and life.

Why do we need to gaslight and manipulate ourselves into thinking things aren't so bad? It's easier than the alternative. It's easier than the fight we believe we would be up against (the perpetrator possibly turning to violence) and allows us to get off relatively unharmed or at least on a physical level. Yet, the challenge is, the more we allow these incidents to go on, we are allowing them on a certain level. We are allowing these behaviors to continue, the patriarchy to continue holding power over women—and the cycle perpetuates. What could happen in one or two generations, if we began to demand and expect respect, but in a feminine compassionate way?

Intuition often begins developing for women in needing to be alert for safety, in all places. Our senses are always honing in on all things, scanning for harm, for issues, and planning ways we will protect ourselves if needed. In essence, we are so often in fight, flight, or freeze, and our nervous systems are on full alert due to it. Creation, compassion, and nurturance, which is the divine essence of women, become really limited in this state. In short, by being in this cycle of different forms of objectification and abuse from men, we are hugely limiting our potential, we are burning ourselves out, and we are passing this way of living on to our daughters.

So, what next? Where do we go from here? I don't like talking about all that is wrong without contemplating a solution.

Fighting men is not the answer, as they too are wounded and hurt. Toxic masculinity is rampant in our society and from a young age, boys are taught to be tough, not show emotions, that women are weaker, and that they are entitled to certain things. Why don't men raise their children differently to break the cycles? Some do, but in order to recognize and go against conditioning one must be healed enough to do so, but healing and emotions are considered weak. This is what we are up against and how deeply it flows. Raging, without direction and healing, is useless and perpetuates the cycle.

Sacred rage, done with compassion, has the potential to create magic.

The difference? Compassion. Compassion comes with healing and transmuting the pain, releasing the trauma, and reclaiming your power, your vibrancy, and your life-force. Every wound we have energetically creates a vortex that holds our personal power hostage. As we heal, we are able to reintegrate pieces and aspects of ourselves and propel ourselves further. For women, the strength and magic we have within us has the ability to create whatever we focus it on. It is potent.

While we all have our divine magic within us, women literally have the power to create life, and it's so much bigger than what we are conditioned to believe or understand. It goes well beyond birthing children. At many times in history women (and their genitalia) were not only adored but worshiped for their magic, manifesting, and creative forces. The feminine was respected as a fundamental piece of all, without them, there is nothing. Just as, without him, the masculine, there is also nothing.

It is my deep knowing that the rise of the feminine and the dismantling of the patriarchy, while desperately needed, are only one aspect of the solution. As women rise into their power and exude the characteristics of this divine feminine through love, nurturing, and receiving, it will allow our fragmented masculine to heal and rise in support of the feminine, as it was intended. Both internally and externally we all possess both energies. In her fullest expression, a woman allows her man (or men in society or internally) to provide for her through structure and generosity. In this balance, he provides the basis for her to flourish and create. Neither is sustainable without the other and this is what we are seeing in our society. Through a lust for power and through fear, the patriarchy has disrobed the vitality out of a woman and the whole thing has toppled over into a heaping pile of rubble.

As women, it is our place and time to come to a state of vibration and love for all that is. To speak our truth to support the healing of others, but to stay in our ultimate balance of nurturing and compassion. Silenced No More. To refused to be silenced to unite others in our quest and missions.

I struggled to stand in my power for so many years for these reasons. It didn't feel safe. I didn't feel safe. Long after I had been married, even. The deep-rooted fear of being exiled by our communities is one that was created for safety. This fear shows up for those of us who are speaking up, sharing our truth and stories. For many of us in the spiritual community, we add to that our witch persecution wounds, and between it all, it can leave us playing small, not showing up, not speaking our truth, or not feeling good enough or just do enough to get by. It often leaves us unfulfilled, frustrated, and feeling burnt out as we navigate our lives through such a masculine energy that has us pushing, pulling back out of fear, fighting ourselves, and moving back and forth. Just as we get ahead, we sabotage ourselves and fall back, often further back than where we started.

As we lean in and challenge our fears, our subconscious beliefs, our societal norms, and our conditioning, we not only support our journey, but we pave the path that much more for future generations. As a mother of a daughter it is not only my desire, but my duty, to teach her how to move through the world both safe and in her power —speaking her truth and being mindful of dangerous situations, arming her for different scenarios while also teaching her to create change.

I am teaching her about the power of her body, the power of her creation, and the power that resides within her essence. I began when she was an infant; I would speak to her as a sovereign being. I would share with her the proper anatomical names of all her body parts. And, I did not allow her needs, discomfort, or apprehensions to be pushed aside for the sake or pleasure of another. From her first breaths, I taught her to trust her feelings, that she was valid and worthy, and that her needs, wants, and desires were also. How, as a child, could I expect her to push her feelings aside if a relative wanted a hug or if she expressed not feeling right and then suddenly know how to trust those same feelings as an adolescent, teenager, and adult? I couldn't. It's not possible. We are not light switches. We are either accepting of our power, our intuition, and our strength with every facet of our beings or we aren't. Turn that light up bright! Not only can we greatly reduce the risk of sexual abuse and grooming, but those lifelong skills of honed instinctual guidance serve us in every single element of our lives.

Many women come to me after decades of programming—overextending themselves to make others happy, living with fear and oppression, and need help excavating their true essences and potency, and, yet, they stick their children in the same systems that perpetuate these lies and suffocation. Let's stop the cycle and give our next generation of daughters not just a map, but a guide. The potential of a woman, and that of the feminine, is sacred and it's time for us to appreciate ourselves and them as such. It is also time to honor the masculine more deeply, to understand, and to appreciate the much-needed role he is to play in our world. By honoring the healed characteristics of both masculine and feminine and encouraging such in our personal interactions, we are creating the pathway for harmony and balance.

ABOUT THE AUTHOR

JESSICA VERRILL

Jess Verrill is an energetic alchemist, intuitive channel, and USA Today best selling author. As the founder of House of Indigo, a multimedia publishing company, she supports spiritual leaders in sharing their unique gifts and creating a product suite that packages their intellectual property into oracle decks, companion workbooks, and books.

Her skills as an intuitive coach and energetic alchemist support high levels of growth and alignment, while working directly as a channel to her guides. As a life-long learner, she is often immersed in books and classes. Her interests include all aspects of herbalism and flower essences, health, wellness and personal development, spirituality, and enhanced psychic development.

Jess lives in Maine where she and her husband homeschool their daughter and live with their black lab and cat. She loves gardening, communing with nature spirits, hiking, exploring nature, being around water, traveling, and personal development.

Learn more and connect here:

publishing@jessverrill.com
jessverrill.com
house-indigo.com
linktr.ee/jessicaverrill

KIMBERLY BERNEY-BROOKE

THE WILD ONE

Silent is the scream that woke me up at night. Silent is the sun as it rises in the morning. Silent is the heart that glimmered anew as I wailed my way into a new world with a slap on my bum and a prick on my foot. The Apgar scores told the staff I was okay.

Are there scores that tell me I am okay as I find my way back to that silent 'glimmering anew' moment? I walk into the cool moonlight that heals the wounds that the salty tears and the warmth of the sun could never close. I've been coming home to my heart, myself, my wild one.

Blueprints

I am adopted and have two mothers. One mother bonded by blood, and the other through a stroke of a pen. Each bestowed their gifts as a pair. Two stories of pain and fear were bequeathed to me in blueprints. These blueprints mingled and merged to create a fortress design to protect me from the pain that comes from the gap between our deepest desires and the unspoken and often harsh expectations placed on girls, daughters, women, and mothers. My job was to follow these blueprints that would dim the flame of my desires that were tended by my wild one. The fortress would lessen the heartbreak and ache that my mothers knew could happen under the heaviness of the demands of this world.

My birth mother's portion of the blueprint included how she silenced her wild one after running away with her high school sweetheart. He broke her heart in fits of drunken rage. When he realized his mistake, he would apologize and promise the world. There would be a period of reconciliation. I was a result of one of these times. When the drunken rage came back, she feared for my life and returned to her parents. They forced her to decide between being relinquished by them or relinquishing me. She was not prepared to separate from her family again. She surrendered her right to be called my mother and only known as my birth mother.

Through the adoption, my mother took me in as her own. Her part of my blueprint was when she learned to extinguish her flame and squelch her wild one completely. She was forced to hand over her paycheck, among other parts of herself, to the patriarch of her family. She learned to use shame and guilt to build her fortress. She taught me that being born a female placed me in a social class that required me to be silent, well-behaved, and accepting of restrictions and rules that didn't apply to boys. These rules were supposed to protect me from predators and molesters.

My Wild One

My wild one never wanted these blueprints. Being self-possessed, she owns her world and embodies a spirit so radiant and glorious that it fills a room with vibrant energy. The energy she exudes can bring a smile and lightness to those who openly listen and try to understand. She can ravish those who deny her light and energy. When this rejection happens, she refuses to leave. She evokes a rage in them so deep that their eyes lash out in fear, sometimes using their tongues to transmit messages to reprogram or completely decommission her light. My mother used words she had learned intentionally designed to diminish my trust in my wild one and myself.

My wild one spoke a language that was unknown to my mother. The language my wild one spoke was that of justice, pride, and empowerment. There was an ease in her movement within the world. My wild one knew I had a louder voice than the preprogrammed, hypnotic loudspeaker messages that played in my head. The messages that are part of the blueprints. Unlike me, she never gave in to those messages. I was lulled and convinced to turn away from her to protect us. I would bring those messages into my head and play them as loud as possible.

She would erupt in rage when the cacophony of the messages was too loud. My body would release her unexpected explosion taking me from zero to one hundred. The heat of her fury flowed from my spine, directly from my amygdala, which had so little control. All I could do was flail in uncontrollable animalistic terror. In my wake, I would leave collateral damage of fear and hurt feelings. I did not have anyone around to help me recognize what was happening.

My wild one rarely felt feelings other than rage and exuberance. Flicking away all other emotions like pesky flies. She fortified herself against the injustices and the lies shared as self-evident truths. My wild one found places to hide away where I could still hear her whispering, but I rarely listened. However, I let her continue to rage through my body.

I saw other girls who were the faithful, cheerful, and well-behaved daughters like my mother longed for. I tried to be that agreeable girl and to grow into a pleasant woman. I tried not to make waves and support others' desires and wishes. This reality would only be possible if I reined in my wild one and followed those blueprints I was given. So, I tried. I really tried.

I kept following those blueprints designed to protect and contain my wild one from the harm of the world. To protect her from the hurt and pain she was feeling. I wanted to quiet the dissonance of sounds in her head—my head.

I worked hard. I followed the blueprints that taught me to clip my wings and bite my tongue. I wasn't very good at it because I would miss parts. The harsh words would slip. I would flap uncontrollably, trying to fly across the room in anger and frustration. My wild one would then unleash the power of her fiery voice that put me into a whirlwind in hopes that someone would listen and understand the messages she had for me.

It took so much effort to silence the screams of my wild one. I tried again to follow those blueprints. To be an obedient daughter, wife, and mother. I took those blueprints and attempted to decipher the symbols that contained the specifications. Still, whenever I set out to follow the instructions, I would get bored and start something new. The structures I started would pulverize into fine grains of sand that, somehow, I would be grinding between my teeth.

Soon I would learn that these blueprints and messages were only an illusion, and they couldn't really protect me.

When Things Changed

The summer between first and second grade was lonely. My family moved back to the town and the house we had left the previous fall. We left to chase my dad's dream to run his own restaurant. We moved to a little town where the restaurant was located.

In that small town, we lived in a house built into the side of a hill with a corrugated tin roof. Cows would walk across that roof as they went to pasture and we would hear the clomping of their hooves. The house would leak whenever there was rain. The school bus would pick us up and drop us off at school, where I felt a sense of safety and warmth. My wild one showed her wonder as that first-grade class watched caterpillars turn into butterflies. The sun shone on my face as the butterflies gathered their courage to fly away in the field outside the school. I imagined them waving goodbye and appreciating the care our class gave them. I didn't have to rush through my schoolwork for playtime as I did in the school I would return to. The rules felt fair and straightforward.

The restaurant didn't last, and we returned to the town we had left. My wild one was back on edge; she missed the magic, exploration, and freedom of that other place.

The house we moved back to had two floors and no central air conditioning. My bedroom was on the second floor, directly above my parent's room. During the summer, window air conditioners were put in my parent's bedroom, the living room, and the small family TV room. Since the upstairs was uncomfortably hot, most summer evenings, my siblings and I would sleep downstairs in the family or living room. We would make forts with sheets and fans. The fan would be pulling in the cold air conditioned air that provided a cocoon to sleep in that staved off the humidity of the midwestern summer heat.

That summer, I was lonely and craved attention. I remember my uncle staying with us and bringing a friend with him. A friend who knew how to prey on lonely and misunderstood children. He paid attention to me. He treated me as if I were seventeen, not the seven-year-old I was. He flattered and listened to me. My wild one was wondering what was happening and was on alert but enjoyed the attention.

One evening, my uncle's friend gave me more attention than I could understand. It felt uncomfortable and gross. My siblings and I were watching TV. I don't have a memory of where my parents or my uncle were. I remember the hard spot in the friend's lap. He wanted me to sit on it. It felt like a rock. I wriggled forward to slide off that rock and sit in front of him on the floor. He would let me be for a bit, then reach out and pull me back. I didn't like that hard thing. He whispered something into my ear with his hot breath, and his arms squeezed me closer to his chest. I didn't understand. I only wanted to watch TV.

Blueprint Failure

"Kim, you need to sleep in my room tonight," my mom insisted in a hushed voice.

"Why?"

Leaning in, my mom whispered in my ear, "That man is trying to get into your panties."

Confused, I asked, "Can't I just sleep in my room and lock the door?"

"No, you need to sleep in my room," she said emphatically.

I was not comfortable in my parent's bedroom. I never felt at home or like I was welcome.

After several rounds, my mom and I compromised, and I slept outside her bedroom door, on the living room floor

That night was restless. I didn't sleep well. My uncle's friend made his way next to me outside my parent's bedroom door. He was doing something I did not understand. I felt him pull my underwear down in the back. My mom came out of her bedroom, and he stopped and slowly removed his hand from my butt.

In a hushed angry voice, my mom would say, "You need to stop that."

There was no response. The silence was broken by my mom's exasperated exhale. She stood there for a bit longer and then returned to her room.

I felt scared. I didn't know what was happening and what exactly my mom wanted to be stopped. I knew my uncle's friend was somehow trying to touch my butt. It felt weird.

Several minutes passed, and he moved closer to me again. My mom came out.

"You need to move to the TV room. You cannot sleep here."

Again, it was silent.

"I know you are not asleep. You need to move."

Her words were addressed by silence and defiance. I felt scared and unsafe.

My mom continued this vigil until it was time to wake up. I had a fitful sleep. I felt I had done something wrong and that I was bad.

Later that summer, after his visit, my family drove on long stretches of highway with few cars around. We didn't wear seatbelts then. The radio was on, and I was sitting in the middle seat when I overheard my parents whisper his name. It caught my attention.

Leaning onto the front seat, I asked, "Who were you talking about?"

"No one." my mom responded.

In my adult mind, I recall something about him being arrested for being a pedophile.

My seven-year-old self asked, "What does that mean?"

"Nothing." Another reply that seemed to tell me I needed to pay attention.

Raging

I forgot about that summer until I was in seventh grade. There was an assembly about sexual assault and abuse. The messages in that assembly stirred the forgotten memory about that creepy mystery man trying to get into my panties and molest me. Memories started to unfold as I was walking home from school after that assembly. Although I was completely safe, I had an unsettling feeling that I was being watched.

My wild one started to rouse from her slumber. She had been very quiet. Something in the messages of that assembly made me realize that my mother's blueprints would not protect me. That the protective fortress was isolating, allowing shame and guilt to fester in the dank corners.

In the following years, my rage became more palpable as my wild one recognized what had happened. My wild one took every opportunity to release a primal scream, throw chairs, kick my foot through the door where my sister was hiding, and punch the wall. All this was because I had closed her off, and she was not heard. I had somehow built a fortress that silenced her in my head, but not in my body. I did not understand what she wanted. Her social justice and empowerment language were lost on me.

Transformation

The memory of that summer slowly came back in glimpses of

images and fragments of conversations. The first piece was my mom whispering, "That man is trying to get into your panties." Other parts came to the surface, creating a path of broken pieces of the story that I tried to put together and make sense of. But it's still not entirely in the frame. The fragments I have don't always fit, and gaps are left in my memory. Over the last few years, I have shared this story with my siblings and asked if they remembered the creepy man. They do.

When I share this story now, people ask, "Why didn't your mom kick the guy out?"

I have been struggling for years with that question and have no answers. My mom could have taken different actions. She had the power to demand the pedophile leave our home rather than having an argument about where my seven-year-old self should sleep. I am beginning to understand that my mom only understood that protection meant locking me away, which was why she had wanted me in her room.

It took me years to understand that she had believed this was enough to protect me. The cages, the towers, and the fortresses are designed to protect the occupant. They are designed to keep those we love safe, like the cages that protect divers from sharks. However, I learned that predators could get inside these protections, which are only shadows. It also means, I don't have to sit waiting for someone to release me. I've been able to walk out all along.

Understanding

Sitting side by side with my mom, I saw the sad helplessness in her eyes. I saw the lost little girl in her. She has learned not to ask for help. My mom always gives and gives but does not receive in return. That was my mother: the one that reared me.

I first noticed this pattern when my dad was in the hospital, delirious and out of sorts. My mom was helpless and scared, unsure of what to do. She kept asking questions that I did not know the answers to. But then she would forget to ask the doctors or the insurance the same questions.

Seeing her in this vulnerable state, I realized she was only doing what she knew. At that moment, I knew my role was to love her, to keep her in my heart, to support her in asking for the help she needed rather than wishing for it to come to her. It was scary to let go of the years of hurt that had caused so much pain and learn how to forgive to forge a new path.

I have burned the old blueprints with the fiery rage of my wild woman. I now have a set of blueprints I want to share for those ready to be freed, for those wanting to find a part of their mother they can hold and love profoundly while watching the hurt, ache, and batterings slip away.

I know I am a product of both my mothers. I am connected through a lineage formed in their wounded wombs. I am invited to break the legacy that has been left to me for my children. I don't want them to shape-shift inside of themselves, to be small, silent, and contorted. The instructions I was bequeathed were crafted for my protection. This protection is only an illusion. All it has done is confined and transformed me into a creature who didn't listen to my heart.

I am walking into a moment that glimmers anew, taking my pulse, checking my color. Telling myself, I am okay. I am now a student of my wild one's language. I invite you to join me on this journey. To realize the cages we have been using as a shield are only shadows; an illusion that keeps us inside. Let's walk outside together to take our first breath of life, again.

ABOUT THE AUTHOR

KIMERLY BERNEY-BROOKE

Kimberly Berney-Brooke is reconnecting to her inner wild one and listening to the lessons she has to offer. As a dancer and a poet, Kimberly enjoys exploring ways to bring these two loves together. She plans to start a practice of healing through bodywork and movement. She wants to study and develop movement practices that heal our physical and emotional aches and pains. Kimberly is also finishing her master's degree in industrial and organizational psychology. She aspires to change the systemic structures of the outdated workplace to reimagine work environments that create connection and belongingness. She currently lives in Brooklyn, New York, with her artist husband and the fun parent, Theodore, and their children, Nathaniel (aka Raine or Brooke), and Winslow.

Learn more and connect here:
www.linkedin.com/in/kimberneybrooke/

https://www.instagram.com/kbb_brooklyn/
https://www.facebook.com/UnevenSurfacesBK/
Unevensurfacesbk@gmail.com

LIZ ZULLI

SALVATION

At age ten, I was looking in the mirror with hate at my reflection. I stared at my body in disgust, pointing out every part I wished was different. I remember running my fingers over my nose knowing the exact spot I would get shaved down for it to look perfect. Most of those moments ended with me in tears after telling myself I was ugly, fat, stupid, and not good enough. There was no understanding of self-love in my young mind, and I wasn't taught it. For years, I blamed my mother. I told myself it should have been her responsibility.

I've since learned there are no "shoulds" in life. Unfortunately, she had a lot of unhealed traumas she carried with her when she became a mother. She wasn't taught to love herself either. During this time, I was bullied by a girl I thought was my best friend. I would come home from school crying and beg my mom to let me transfer schools. My bedroom quickly became a haven. It was a creative haven for me to isolate myself from the world. I would turn to visual art and writing in my journals as an outlet for my pain. I started to ask questions like, Who am I? Do people even see me? Would it matter if I disappeared? But I didn't know how to effectively communicate what I was feeling. When I did share my thoughts and emotions I felt invalidated and as if my emotions were too much. I felt like I was a burden. Deep down what I did know to be true about myself was that I had a kind heart, but my life was headed down a self-destructive path.

My mental health issues started to run my life. I was grappling with feelings I couldn't put into words. I was experiencing overwhelming fear in the form of anxiety and depression. I developed an eating disorder in my teen years due to trauma and a lack of self-love. In high school, I experienced battles with anorexia and bulimia convinced that they would make me attractive and love myself. All I thought about was my body and the way it looked. I believed that my worth was measured by my appearance. This embedded belief system led me to look for other forms of love in all the wrong places. I was addicted to the idea of finding love, trying to fill a void with anything external. I thought if guys were attracted to me then that must mean I'm "enough." It was the bad boys who caught my eye and my hormones. Jumping from relationship to relationship, I never spent time being single to try to build an intimate relationship with myself or to cultivate the love that was missing within me. It was a perpetuated cycle of wounds I collected over the next fifteen years.

Flash forward to my freshman year of college, I mindfully started to transform my life. It was like a switch had been turned on. I was ready to end the self-sabotaging thoughts about my body image and act. It all had to start within my mind. I started to focus on the foundation of my well-being. I read personal development books. I discovered a new passion for fitness and nutrition and it soon became the way in which I gained confidence, discipline, and a healthier mindset about myself. Life was great. I had a healthier relationship with my body and food. I was hitting the gym five days a week and even started a handmade jewelry business. I was set up for the best four years of my life!

Then, something happened.

Shortly after my new lifestyle plan started, my family shattered. I found myself without the excitement of college. I was lost. My two unhealthy parents got to a place in their marriage where one decision changed the course of our family; I wasn't surprised. Based on what I had experienced love to mean while growing up, I learned love meant invalidation, comparison, belittling, materialism, and not creating or respecting boundaries. There were some healthy ways love was shown, such as providing basic needs, creating experiences through travel, and praise of accomplishments. I learned from my parents what to do and what not to do. My heart had a gaping void for love and family.

A lot of my weekends during my college years were spent sacrificing my time and energy to support my mother whose health took a drastic turn because of the state of her marriage. It appeared me and my mother's roles had switched. I became the parent and she became the child. It felt like I lost my childhood and young adult years. Throughout college, I ended up in romantic relationships with toxic partners that I craved love from. They were emotionally unavailable, but I needed a challenge, a project, because I was a fixer.

In my sophomore year, I dated someone who was the first person I felt spiritually connected to and he was a recovering drug addict. But one vivid night, we fought and he said, "This is codependent." meaning us. I can still hear him say it as he walked out my bedroom door. That was the first time I heard the word, and it went way over my head. It wasn't until ten years later that I learned what it meant.

In my senior year, I met a guy from college (who later became my husband) while my world felt like it was falling apart. I had never been more in love. He was my rock during the family turmoil. This relationship woke me up for good and allowed me to come face to face with all my uncomfortable truths. One of the biggest truths was I passed the responsibility to everyone, except me, to heal and create happiness for myself.

In 2013, I lost my mother: the woman who didn't know how to empower me but gave me life and many blessings. A year and a half later, I got married, and in 2015, I received one of the best gifts, my daughter. Some mothers say it's the best year of their life, being pregnant; that was not the experience I had. There I was with the positive pregnancy test in my hand, and in another unhealthy relationship, in which I felt trapped, realizing I had just become a motherless mother.

It was the most painful feeling, aside from losing my mom. I felt completely lost and helpless, with only one family member close by, and very few loved ones knowing what was going on at the time.

I became a girl hiding behind a smile on social media, fighting anxious thoughts daily, and losing what I thought was my identity at the time. I minimized my traumatic experiences in my relationship to give myself a false sense of protection and holding onto glimpses of hope that we would be restored to the happy couple we once were. I kept thinking this was not what I wanted and not what my daughter deserved.

The whole time I was blinded by my own pain. I didn't see my own contribution in the marriage. I didn't see that I had brought all my unhealed trauma into what I fantasized would be the most beautiful, committed relationship of my life. I was still that little girl desperate for attention, love, and validation, and I was grieving from loss. I entered the marriage with a fantasy; it would be completely different from my parent's marriage. I put an expectation on my partner that he was there to save me and be the man I needed since my father wasn't, but also having the empowering energy that my mother didn't provide. I was a girl with a big void. I had a picture in my mind of what I wanted things to look like and believed they should be. The reality was one of my worst nightmares was about to come true —divorce.

Uncertainty and fear were magnified and I made the choice to say, enough is enough. I simply could not take it anymore. My daughter needed a healthy mom who stood up for herself. I was finally ready to break my patterns of trauma and suffering. From having my family broken apart to losing my mother to being in an unhealthy marriage, something had to change. That something was me. I had clarity that a lot of my situations were a result of how I was showing up in my life, but I wasn't clear on why. With every ounce of my being, I was determined to discover why. I wanted a new life. I had to unlearn and then relearn. I had to be ready to unpack everything that created my mindset and circumstances up to that point. The only way out was through the dark.

During this transition, I was greatly affected by substance abuse and it led me to seek answers. God placed two friends in my life who shared the opportunity of Al-Anon with me. From that moment on, my life was never the same again. Al-Anon is a recovery program for friends and family who are affected by alcoholism. I entered recovery thinking I was going to learn all about the person with alcoholism and I quickly discovered that I was about to get to know myself. I discovered my addiction was codependency. I checked all the boxes: people pleaser, poor self-esteem, lacking boundaries, reactive, poor communicator, and caretaker. What a beautiful wakeup call. It was the beginning of shedding an identity that no longer served me. I was ready to dive as deep as I could to save my inner child, to see her, feel her, and tell her that it's time she came out of hiding. She could put out her arms and receive love and freedom again.

I traveled back in time starting with the very first painful thing I remembered being said to me and every painful event that had shaped me up to this point. I had embarked on a healing journey of release, recovery, and rebirth. It was emotional freedom that I desired, and I was ready to be the mother I envisioned for my daughter. I made it an everyday mission to be a conscious parent, and to be intentional with repairing my mind, body, and spirit so she did not have to repeat my patterns. Our children watch and listen to everything we do. Trauma is inherited, but we get the choice to end the cycle and start anew. We get to be the leaders for them and pave the way.

Over the past three years in Al-Anon, I have experienced immense spiritual awakenings that expanded my consciousness to the truth of my real identity as a child of God. I grew up with a strong intuition and connection to God, but this was different on a level than I could have imagined. I grew a personal relationship with my Higher Power. My identity was no longer defined by my old thought patterns, mistakes, relationships, jobs, personal style, or lifestyle. Nobody could ever love me as much as God. My worth can never be negotiated.

Through recovery, one of the biggest lessons I learned was surrender. In the beginning I was surrendering with desperation. It wasn't until I moved further into my journey that I began to understand the true meaning of surrender and what happens when we consciously choose it. It was a release. A release of the old life. I released old harmful thought patterns; like if I looked a certain way, I would be loved more. I discovered that when people do not see my worth or they hurt me it does not define me. I created a new internal world which in turn created a new external world. Everything I thought I knew about love and relationships shifted.

For me to stay committed to my healing journey without distractions, I had to not repeat my pattern of jumping into other relationships after my divorce. I stayed single and focused on myself for four years except for a brief three-month long relationship that I had to disengage from to refocus on my recovery program. I took myself on solo adventures and dates. There is something empowering about saying, "Table for one." I learned how sacred the relationship with myself is. It took work. It is a daily decision to choose me.

I opened myself up and dismantled every false belief I ever had before I understood the root of each and why I allowed them to keep me in pain. I learned that in exploring the depths of my past pain I, too, have turned to substances to escape and to cope. I tried to compare my shortcomings with others, especially those who engaged in alcohol. However, I learned there's no scale of comparison and I cannot be the judge or jury for someone else's decisions. I, too, am just human. We are all mirrors for each other, experiencing the same emotions throughout life with different, but sometimes related stories. We all need love and want to belong. When we don't have a conscious personal relationship with our Higher Power, we look externally for things to fill that need for love.

The result of me intentionally choosing to show up for myself and take the path I'm on has given me an extraordinary rebirth. I'm eager to start each day not knowing what will come my way, because I know whatever does I will get through it. With the strength of God, I've gone from a girl who didn't want her life to a girl who has completely and utterly fallen in love with herself and the life she has created so far.

I've accepted my humanness in being vulnerable enough to share the deepest darkest pieces of me because I know my story will help others. I give myself permission to be my imperfect authentic self. I'm a healed empath knowing how to understand and regulate emotions whereas before I was ashamed of my emotions and let them drive my life. I learned that I don't need to control things, people, or situations to protect myself. I am protected.

I've been given the gift of salvation. Every part of me is worthy and enough in the eyes of God. No one can ever take that away from me or stop me from being loved and living in joy. I am free. Free from the shame, guilt, and resentment that weighed on me ever since I was a child. I have forgiven the little girl who looked in the mirror with hate and who self-sabotaged herself for over twenty years. I have forgiven those who hurt me when they were hurting. I can lay my troubles down at any given moment and surrender because I am safe and loved. I walk in faith now—not in fear.

Our experiences here on earth are not for us. They are for the next person who needs to hear them to feel loved, seen, understood, validated, enough, and not alone. We go through life thinking our experiences are unique and incomparable. We are never alone, and God reminds us of that through using our stories to connect and heal one another.

God is always within and around waiting for us to say we're ready. I continue to listen to the spiritual nudges every day leading me further into my purpose. It's a beautiful thing to give ourselves permission to heal and to determine how we want our hearts to feel every day. If we give others the responsibility of filling our voids, we will be disappointed. Our lives are our responsibility. How healed and happy we choose to be is our choice. When we heal the dark, the emerging light creates a ripple effect on those around us. That can only begin when we start the inner work of creating a loving relationship with ourselves. We do not have to merely survive. We do not have to hold ourselves hostage to our desires for an abundant life. We are not our parents and their parents. We are not what happened to us or the stories we tell ourselves, and we can stop the pattern of pain holding us back from love, joy and connection.

To the beautiful being reading this—you are a masterpiece with an unfinished story. Choose you. Choose your healing. You matter, your voice matters, your words have power, so let the world hear you. Own your story and who you are!

I want to see more women standing up for themselves and raising up other women. I want my daughter to see the impact of women rising together and for her to create that for her generation. I don't want any woman to waste any more of her life as a victim of her circumstances or the limiting beliefs she tells herself. There is another way to live, a better one.

I wouldn't be where I am today in love with my life if it weren't for God. I'm grateful for all my experiences that have led me to a place where I can support others along their path. What I realized throughout my journey of healing over the past four years is that I was never lost, I was exactly where I was meant to be all along, and my eyes have been opened to see that I was just being found.

For my daughter and for all the women who stay silent with a lioness voice roaring inside not knowing she is worth it to let it out. Let your voice echo into the mountains and valleys creating ripples of courage, love, and hope for generations to come.

"Every woman who heals herself, helps heal all women who came before her, and all those who will come after." – Dr. Christiane Northrup

ABOUT THE AUTHOR

LIZ ZULLI

Liz is an intuitive visual storyteller who loves to celebrate people's transformations through her photography. She has a bachelor's degree in business management from West Chester University that she used to develop her former handmade jewelry business, ZULLI Designs, and now focuses on expanding her photography business, Liz Zulli Photography. Liz has a deep love for new experiences through insatiable wanderlust, tastes, and encounters with strangers. Nature is her happy place. She is a mother, empath, and visionary who turned pain into purpose with a mission to show her daughter and other women how cultivating self-love creates a life of joy, connection, and freedom. Liz empowers women to step out of their comfort zone and into their power by capturing images of their authentic selves.

Learn more and connect here:

https://www.facebook.com/LizZulliPhotography
https://www.instagram.com/Zulliphotography/
LizZulliPhotography@gmail.com

LOVELLA S. MAXEY

FOUND IN SILENCE

I sat and spoke to those around me, telling them what I dream to be, explaining the drive that led me to what I see, and the map that will guide me there. I had so much excitement and cheer in my voice, that anyone listening would know it was what was destined to be. I would sit listening intently to the advice that was being given about life, grasping at every syllable, clutching to every punctuation, clasping to every subject, noun, verb, and predicate not wanting to miss any pertinent information.

When I went to open my mouth to respond to the words of wisdom I had just received, nothing comes out. I tried again. I could see my lips moving, but no sound comes out. Everything around me was now silent. I was panicked, confused, and unsure of where I was. I braced myself, took a deep breath, closed my eyes, opened my mouth, and screamed as loud as I could: a silent scream. Though no sound came out, I could still feel the fire in my chest and the embers dancing in my throat. Through my closed lids, a single tear began to fall.

I opened my eyes. I stared blankly at the sunset painted on the wall across from me wondering what my mother would think of this situation if I told her, but I quickly brushed the thought off. I knew she was rolling over in her grave with what she saw. I imagined the possible ways I could fight back and the possible outcomes if I did. My thoughts were broken when I heard, "Does it hurt?" I turned my attention away from watching the yellow blended orange with a hint of pink blended purple stacked horizontally by the sunset illuminating the living room like a movie scene. My gaze was met with a grimaced smile. I gave a solemn and melancholy "No." as a response. "I can make it hurt," he said with a slight smile. I ignored his response. As my eldest brother continued to thrust himself into my body, I went back to looking at the painting God gave me to ease my mind in my time of need.

I tried my hardest to escape into the painted sunset, but it was the real-life sunset that sent me into the darkness I awoke into. I began to question everything: how could God create something so beautiful that it could ease my mind, yet he couldn't do anything to help me escape the physical pain? How could my mother give birth to a man who was so evil and filled with nothing but darkness? I witnessed how inhumanely he would treat his girlfriend. Beating her in front of his child, and later kick the child out of the room to be cared for by me, his freighted fourteen-year-old sister. He'd treat his own child as if he had no relation to her. He would force her mother to be her sole physical provider after a brutal attack, and in the same breath, threaten to kill her if she were to ever try to take her from him. He loved his child so much that he named her after a character in his favorite movie, Higher Learning.

However, only a month after my arrival, he was willing to use his daughter and I as hostages should the police be called after he beat his girlfriend in the car on the way to work for suspected cheating before kicking her out of the car miles away from home and work. He left his girlfriend stranded and beaten, rushed home to barricade the doors, and began pulling out handguns and assualt riffles, he was ready to go to war with the police and take us down with him. As I watched and listened to him talk to his panicked girlfriend on the phone, he ensured to tell her "Bitch I don't give a fuck about you. Call the police if you want to. It's gone be a shoot out in this bitch. You not taking my child from me."

I spent too much time in my world of escape and now I was forced to endure every moment of this pain, counting every drop of his sweat that falls on me, feeling every time my head hits the leather arm of the couch, and wondering when he'll be done so I could run away. I was consumed by thoughts, recounting each time he had raped me and the moments leading up to it. I wondered if what was happening to me was my fault. He was not the first but I prayed he was the last. I forced myself to be a martyr (I had already died many times over), but maybe in sacrificing myself this time, it'd be for a good cause. Maybe, I could save his girlfriend from some of the harsh blows she faced from a man who was supposed to be my brother.

He would tell me that we are not kin, "half-siblings don't count." The womb we shared only mattered for him. Who was once our mother, was now only his mother, because he was born first. Maybe it was his way of disassociating himself from what he was doing to me or more so whom he was doing things to. Because if he didn't see me as his little sister, he could see me as his secret girlfriend. And I said nothing in protest.

Time seemed to go on endlessly and I felt as though he would never finish. He asked another question and I'm pulled from my thoughts. "Does it feel good?" I was so afraid to speak; I was unsure if I should lie and say yes or be honest and tell him no. I didn't want to encourage the behavior, but I was too afraid to see what the truth would get me. I just stared at him trying to speak because even the idea of not saying anything struck fear into my heart.

There was a knock at the door. I was saved by interruption; he jumped to put his pants back on while I scurried from underneath him to do the same. I ran to open the door. It was the little girl from downstairs. Maybe, it was God's intervention or maybe it was just a coincidence, but I didn't care, I was just happy to be saved. She was there visiting her dad and wanted to know if I could come out to play. I closed the door and went to him. "That's Tasha. Can I go outside with her?" I waited with anticipation, trying to put on a brave face as I watched him look me up and down. He sat on the couch as he lit a Newport cigarette. He took a puff of his cigarette and looked at it to verify it was lit. "Yeah, you can go." I exclaimed "Thank you; thank you; thank you!" and ran to safety.

As hard as it felt to find things I had in common with this girl, she was my safe zone. She was the only person I was able to hang out with, with no questions or fuss from my brother. I think that was because her father and my brother were friends. But whatever the reason, I was determined to hold on to her and take any and every opportunity provided to get out of that apartment. Though it wasn't often I got to hang out with her, she always seemed to come around at the best of times. Like when I really felt as though I needed saving, and I was forever grateful for that.

We would stay outside for a little while. We'd sit in the parking lot talking about our week at school, events going on, things we wanted to do, things we wanted to buy, boys, and how we were so happy that school was almost over before we would head downstairs to her apartment. There I was surrounded by people who seemed to care for each other, but I wasn't fooled. I knew nothing was ever as great as it seemed. But at least in her house I never had to be subjected to the things I was at my home. It was perfect for me.

I never knew how to disrupt the peace I experienced in their home. I never knew how to break the ice to ask for help. I would always tell myself that I would do it when I was presented with the opportunity to do so: like if they were to ask me, "How is everything at home?" or "Do you feel safe at home?" Or, maybe, we would be having a random conversation about someone else, and I would just throw myself into the conversation and, nonchalantly, mention it in a way that would force them to ask questions.

But, in reality, I knew I would never say anything because I was afraid and not ready to deal with the confrontation of how everything could possibly play out. I was especially not ready to face the possibility of if I wasn't believed, because then what would happen to me? What would happen to them if they ever confronted him? Would I end up back with my abuser? What would that mean for his girlfriend and daughter? The possibility of being believed was not worth putting everyone in a life-or-death situation when I had no evidence or knowledge on ensuring the truth meant it'd be believed.

It has been almost a full year since my first day arriving in Seattle, Washington. It was fear, confusion, and love that engulfed my mind, body, and soul. I didn't know what to make of the abuse I endured. Was it really happening to me again? Was it my fault? Did I deserve this life? With so many similar instances of being raped, molested, and sexually harassed, I felt like this was the life I was destined for. I gave no protest a year prior about moving with my brother when my Auntie Momma found out I was speaking out against her, and saying hurtful things like wishing death upon her to my supposed friends in a fit of anger because she was speaking truths to me about my mother that my child-like mind was not ready to hear or accept as truth.

I never asked or wanted to be relocated. I was told that I would be. My venting turned into a lifetime of trauma and mistrust, all because I did not speak out in protest to her when she said that I no longer wanted to be with her when I knew I did. My issues with my Auntie Momma went deeper than the angry things I spoke about towards her. There was a conversation that needed to be had, and it didn't happen until years later when it was no longer relevant or able to preserve the little bit of innocence that remained within me at thirteen-years-old, before my departure.

Two months after the interrupted rape, my abuser was arrested for a crime unrelated to either of us. During his absence, his girlfriend and I had a conversation about how calm everything in the house had been with him being locked away and how free we felt to speak. As we talked, she reassured me she would never go back to him and how foul his actions were to not only her, but to us as a family. She began to tell me of all of the horrendous acts he had committed before I arrived and after. Like how he once beat our mother because he found out she was prostituting herself for money and drugs or how on Mother's day he beat his girlfriend mercilessly while I tended to his oldest child (from a previous relationship) who had come over to visit and his youngest, daughter. As I heard her recount the events, all I could hear was the screaming, yelling, banging, death threats, and pleading that came from beyond the bedroom door as I held both children who buried their heads in my chest crying. She recounted events from her side of the door and I replayed the sounds I heard from my side of the door. Eventually, our stories get to a point where they match up and my brother walked out of the room with a bloody hand and left the house for hours, but she had remained in the bedroom for an extended period after he had left. He had cut his hand on a large suitcase he had thrown at her and blamed her for cutting his hand, so he choked her until she passed out before leaving the house. I stared in shock as I listened on while she put the final nail in the coffin. The last part of her account of that night was her telling me she miscarried due to the extensive beating. It broke my heart because I understood her views on having kids; she cherished them and loved being pregnant. Because of the miscarriage, she held firm on taking this opportunity to run away and never look back. I applauded her for her courage. Regardless, I needed to add my own nail to the coffin, so I told her about him using me as an excuse to go out and cheat with another woman and as I explained this she looked mortified and angry. I could see all the wheels turning in her head as she started to spout out all the pieces she started to put together. I cared nothing about what she was saying. I was more excited to see her anger and hear her plans to escape.

I figured the confirmation of his infidelity would help to make sense of why a lot of her beatings came from his insecurities about his cheating and thinking she was doing the same. As much as I saw it coming, my heart raced when I heard her ask me if he had abused me in any manner. I looked at her with what I could only imagine was a terrified expression on my face, but I tried to pass it off as a look of shock. As if to say, how dare she have the audacity to ask me such a question. I figured putting the pieces together of our cruel life and finally having a space to talk about it was more than enough. I didn't need to share that with her. I didn't need to tell her about the conversation about me being his secret girlfriend, though I was the "other woman," I wasn't the only woman. I didn't need to tell her about him planning to pimp me out, or how he pistol whipped me ever so slightly the night she went to the hospital for her miscarriage, or even the accounts of rape that ensued before, during, and after that night. I chose to remain silent as I believed my days of being a martyr were finally coming to an end and my secret was able to die with me. She had experienced enough pain dealing with that narcissistic raging psychopath.

Too many injustices filled that small apartment even before I arrived into my brother's care; twenty-four hours after my arrival the walls began to witness even more injustices being served. If walls could talk, they would cry until the paint ran off, before they would be able to recount anything that happened; they would let out a bellow so loud it would do nothing but shake the foundation of the ground it stood on. With all the pain they've witnessed, the hard blows of bodies, objects, and fists, and the pain that they, themselves have felt along with the blood and tears they've felt run down their cold, off-white exterior they would weep. During the year I stayed with my brother, it felt like a glimpse of eternal damnation but I survived. Though I self harmed during my time with him in order to feel that I was still alive. I tried to hang myself in order to not endure the pain he left me with but I survived. I know now that if not only did I place my own nail in the coffin but buried the coffin myself, the feelings of anger, despair, loneliness, fear, grief, depression, and confusion that I carried from fourteen-years-old until I was twenty-six-years old, would not have been so grave to my journey into adulthood. Had I not waited until I was twenty-two-years old to let go of a secret that was not mine to keep. If I had spoken out sooner and dealt with the discomfort of speaking about the events that took place sooner, I could have gotten help and been on the road to recovery sooner. Yet, hindsight is 20/20 and I began my recovery at twenty-two years old and healed at twenty-six because I was found in my silence.

ABOUT THE AUTHOR

LOVELLA S. MAXEY

Lovella Maxey is a phenomenal public speaker and author. She has risen above adversity and hardships. Despite it all, she relentlessly shows kindness and compassion toward others while motivating them to overcome their trauma. She understands the healing process and encourages them as they go through it to take small steps.

Lovella was a phlebotomist for two years, serving in the US Army for four years,graduated college, and became a veteran. She is currently working in Human Resources while pursuing her dreams of becoming an author, public speaker and life coach. A dream that will soon become her reality.

Learn more and connect here:
https://www.instagram.com/soulfulpoet95/
lsmssc9519@gmail.com

MEGAN BARNHARD

SOME BODY TO LOVE

"If you're going to give up anyway, you might as well do exactly what you want."
~ Laís Scort

I'm twenty-six. I'm locked in the bathroom of my apartment. From the other side of the door, someone has just asked the scariest question I can imagine: "What do you want?"

* * *

I WAS three years old when I first experienced eight thousand nerve endings in my Radiance, my most sacred place, lighting up with an intensity unlike anything else in my short life up until then. I was lying on the floor of the treehouse in our backyard. The older girls in the neighborhood were letting me play with them. They were my heroes, and I craved their love and acceptance more than anything. Here they were, giving me their rapt attention. All I had to do was lie on my back on the AstroTurf floor and allow them to take turns pressing into me with their bodies. It was wonderful to be the center of attention, yet unsettling because my body knew something didn't feel right. There was an air of secrecy and shame. I knew, intuitively, that if I told anyone what was happening, the older girls would get in trouble, and they would blame me.

This is my earliest memory of life being a balancing act. Of trying to predict what would make other people happy so that they would accept me, include me, want me. And of ignoring my own intuition in order to try to please others.

I kept the treehouse secret, but the older girls left me behind anyway, despite my silence. It was simply the natural course of growing up: they didn't want to play with the little kid anymore. For me, it was devastating. I felt they were rejecting me and my most intimate parts. I believed they'd used me and thrown me away.

The lesson seemed so clear: connection leads to rejection. Already highly-sensitive, I became anxious and overwrought. My small nervous system went into hypervigilance, always one moment away from terror or tantrum. I was unsafe. Anyone could leave me at any moment, for any reason. I looked for safety in being able to predict the world through rules. Unfortunately, the rules my scared mind invented and held onto with white-knuckled rigidity were the following:

- Anyone who loves me will eventually reject me.
- My body's desires are wrong.
- Receiving attention is dangerous.

THE TREEHOUSE WAS TORN down when we moved, but its impact stayed with me. I remained convinced that those tingling feelings were bad, secret, and shameful. Any time I felt aroused, I felt horribly guilty. Even worse, it was girls who gave me those aroused feelings. If there was one thing I learned from the mean kids at summer camp it was that girls liked boys, and girls who didn't like boys were disgusting. End of story.

I stayed silent about this unbearable feeling in my sacred parts, hoping it would leave me alone. But the feeling was about to get much worse.

* * *

My brain had wired "arousal" and "bad" together. Each time I swelled with sexual arousal, my brain sent back the message "disgusting." The thing about the body and brain, though, is that communication goes in both directions. Soon, the feedback loop began to run the other way: any time I would get disgusted, scared, anxious, or agitated, my Radiance would flood with blood.

As I am a wonderfully sensitive being, my nervous system reacted very strongly to so many stimuli. Just being alive in the world made me feel it all so deeply. I was saddened and disturbed by so much. But even as my mind would feel horror at an image or a story, my body would become engorged.

Oh, Little Megan! Now, as an adult, you know that this is simply over-coupling: the body and brain associating two things so tightly that they lose track of cause and effect. Neurons fire together and become wired together. But you did not know this. You thought you were irrevocably damaged.

My silence became an oppressive presence in my life. I couldn't tell a soul about what was happening to my body. How do you explain that any time there's a very bad man in a movie, and he does a very bad thing, your body reacts as if it's aroused? Or that the soft, sticky sounds of your family eating dinner send you spiraling into a sweaty rage because the misophonic pain registers in your body in the parts meant for feeling pleasure? It was so alienating to remain silent. Yet, it was the only way. Surely, if anyone knew what was happening they would reject and abandon me immediately. Just like the older neighborhood girls had done.

If I spoke up about the feelings, I might also have to break my silence about what I was doing to cope with them.

I don't recall when I started attacking my Radiance by punching and slapping myself. It was the only thing that relieved the swollen feeling and gave me respite from the agony of arousal. I thought I deserved it. I was so bad and so wrong for feeling any desire, let alone this desirous feeling in response to things in the world that disturbed me so deeply.

Guilt that is silenced becomes shame, and shame self-perpetuates. Now a new shame was added to my list. The shame of self-harm. It would be many more years until I broke the silence of my pain and what I was doing in response to it. In the meantime, I managed to push my memories deep, deep down. Forgetting them entirely. I dealt with triggering situations by self-harming or self-leaving: when the world became too intense, I simply dissociated and floated away.

* * *

I WAS fifteen when the memories of the treehouse came flooding back in an overwhelming instant. I was lying on my back in a meadow of dead grass on a cool autumn evening. A boy was kissing me and pressing his body against mine. I was floating above myself, trying not to be there.

Suddenly the feeling of meadow grass poking through my shirt dragged me back to earth. This sensation was all too familiar. I was three again, lying on the AstroTurf floor of the treehouse. Scared, and yet frozen and unable to do anything to stop what was happening.

Around this time, I went through a Model Mugging(™) course where women learned to defend themselves against attackers in padded suits. You could hit, elbow, and yell, "No!" It was meant to be therapeutic and give women a chance to recalibrate their nervous systems by fighting instead of fleeing or freezing in the face of trauma. I ended up shaking, crying, and curling into the fetal position on the floor in every exercise.

With the world so full of threats that sent me into a full-body freeze, I withdrew into my mind. I thought I could live in ideas. I started reading books that reinforced my worldview that emotions were dangerous, only rational thought was important, and you couldn't depend on anyone but yourself. I felt safe in those ideas. They echoed the rules my three-year-old self had made.

That spring, I learned my drama teacher had met the author of the books I was devouring, and I was elated. I started staying after class to discuss big ideas with him. He left Xeroxed copies of lectures for me on the school bulletin board. Finally, someone who wanted to be around me for my mind! Over the summer break, he invited me out to lunch and put his hand between my legs. I was frozen. I left my body once again. Of course. I should have known. I transferred schools to get away from him, but also to get away from my friends. I couldn't be close to people. I retreated further into my mind, ignoring my body and her wisdom.

* * *

I WAS twenty-four when my body was electrified by the most intense physical pain I have ever experienced. Like defibrillation, it was a shock to my system that brought me back from the dead.

I'd become pregnant, despite having been on the pill. I never saw myself as a mom. Never wished for a family. The physical reality of carrying a baby and giving birth was horrifying. I was the person who gagged at the sight of needles, fainted while getting blood drawn, and left my body during routine medical exams. My terror grew when my doctor told me I was Rh negative and would need regular blood draws and injections to have a healthy pregnancy. But that was nothing compared to my fear of becoming a mother. My self-hatred felt like a hereditary disease, and there was no way I was passing it on. All I knew how to do was freeze, whether in the face of danger or someone else's desire. I couldn't protect myself, let alone a defenseless new life.

I was racked with guilt and shame that my life had gone in the wrong direction. What a bad investment I'd been to everyone who believed in me and supported me. Here I was in a job I hated, not living my passions, and now pregnant to top it off. There was no end to my self loathing. Yet, I was certain about my next steps. I knew my decision was absolutely right, despite how absolutely wrong my situation felt.

The termination procedure was like napalm in my womb. There's nothing I've experienced that comes close to that level of pain and sadness. Faced with that intensity, my mind should have been long gone. Dissociation was my number-one skill. I did it during gynecological exams, dental check-ups, and even fast car rides. Yet somehow, I remained in my body. I was clear and cogent throughout the procedure. It was as if I were finally present to protect myself. When it was all over, I felt an expansive calm. I placed my hands over my womb and said to her, "Let's never do this again."

After having so much violence inflicted on my most sacred parts, I began to feel protective of them. This was my body. How could I have treated her so poorly all these years? How could I have let her suffer for my anger, my frustration, my unwillingness to deal with my feelings? I'd had my eyes opened. I no longer wanted to hurt my Radiance. I no longer wanted to feel ashamed of her. I wanted to love myself and be loved profoundly in return.

Exactly nine months after I'd gotten pregnant, I gave birth. Not to a baby, but to a new version of myself. The version of me who could finally ask for what she wanted.

* * *

When we met at an open mic at a coffee shop, I knew this man was for me. For the first time in my life, I took action. Up until then, I'd "ended up" with men, being a passive participant in their desires. Not this time. I boldly gave this guy my number, and we talked on the phone every night for a week about Aristotle and Elvis Costello. I couldn't wait to see him again.

When I did see him, something extraordinary occurred: I swooned. I got tunnel vision and started sweating. The coffee shop full of people disappeared, and he was all I could see. But in all that intensity of feeling, I did not leave my body. I did not dissociate. I stayed right there in that room and allowed my body to lead. She was clearly telling me what she wanted, and I was listening.

He kissed me in a way I'd never been kissed before. My body lit up with pure joy, free from terror, guilt, or shame. I'd never felt so fully present. It was the opposite of dissociating and floating away. It was as if I were alive and on the earth for the first time.

We began dating seriously. I shyly whispered to him about my eight thousand nerves and his eyes lit up. Far from being disgusted, he was eager and excited to send me into waves of ecstasy. My whole life, I'd thought there was something wrong with me. Movies and TV showed women were supposed to feel pleasure just one way, and my way was different. (It would be more than a decade before I'd read that all female orgasms originate in this magical place, and that there's nothing strange about me at all.)

Here I was, asking for what I wanted for my body. My rules were about to be severely challenged. But they wouldn't go without a fight.

* * *

Facing so much happiness, I quickly reached my upper limit. Who was I to feel so good? Who was I to feel physically fulfilled as well as intellectually and emotionally delighted? I began to start fights with this man, projecting onto him my self-hatred. I was daring him to leave with my behavior. After all, I knew it was only a matter of time before connection led to rejection.

Oh, 26-year-old Megan, I see you. You believed so strongly that you would be rejected that you tried to bring it about. You needed the world to be a predictable place and for your rules to be true. You said you would rather be right than happy.

* * *

So, that's where I was, on the other side of the bathroom door, hating and hitting myself, when he asked me that terrifying question: *"What do you want?"*

It had begun as a conversation about how miserable I was at my job, but it had escalated into a fight when he'd encouraged me to quit. I'd insisted I was pathetically un-hirable, and there was nothing other than teaching that I could possibly do in the world. A truth spoken directly from my three-year-old self who felt she was so, so broken.

He leaned close to the bathroom door and said softly, "What do you want so bad that it scares you?"

"To write," I responded without thinking.

"Do you love it?" he asked.

"Yes," I replied quietly.

"Are you willing to compromise?"

"Yes," my soul whispered. I didn't even know what the question meant, yet I somehow knew the answer.

I opened the door. He pulled me into a hug.

I'd shown him all my ugliness and told him all of my secrets. The treehouse. The termination. The self-harm. The tantrums. And he didn't reject me.

In fact, in that moment he was inviting me to stop rejecting myself and to lean into who I truly wanted to be.

A month later I quit my job without knowing what was next. I had only one writing coaching student lined up and no business plan, but I felt so light. I was finally owning what I wanted and going after it with my whole heart.

* * *

REWRITING RULES TAKES TIME. I wish I could say that they were permanently obliterated after I opened the bathroom door. But, darling reader, you're wise enough to know that's not how it works.

I did stop self-harming. I never hurt my Radiance from that day forward. I found amazing professionals to help me on my journey.

I worked with a Somatic Experiencing therapist who taught me how to orient and feel safe in my body. It was with her support that I was able to revisit so much of what had happened to Little Megan and learn to titrate my agitation and arousal. With her help, I stopped picking so many fights with the man I loved, the man who'd asked me what I wanted, because I stopped trying to enforce the rules my three-year-old self had made.

I built on that foundation with an Emotional Freedom Technique (EFT) practitioner who gave me additional tools to allow the big emotions to pass through me without harming me or making me want to harm myself.

These women helped me build the foundation to truly be in my body. I finally gave myself permission to feel my feelings. The more I did that, the more my rules crumbled and turned to dust.

* * *

NINE YEARS after that afternoon in the bathroom, I was sitting in an EFT session and tapping on something particularly frustrating, when my therapist asked in her gentle but authoritative voice, "What would you like to have happen?"

It was like the floor dropped out from under me. But instead of falling into a void, I realized I was floating in infinite possibility. I'd been so caught up in what was happening to me that I hadn't thought to ask what I wanted. This question was a revelation. I remember smiling broadly and easily coming up with an answer. From then on, this question became the fulcrum of our work together. In beautiful confirmation, as I started to name what I wanted, my desires began to flow to me like magic.

Within a few months, my sexy philosopher and I got engaged, something I'd wanted with all my heart but felt was impossible because of my doubts about being a worthy partner.

Shortly after that, I pivoted my writing coaching practice from serving students—thinking that was my only option—to serving business owners and helping them write their stories and share their messages. My heart was lit up and I began to see the true depths of my Story Magician powers.

I had finally learned not to fear my desires, not only the desires of my body, but my visions for my career, and the deep yearnings of my soul. My intuition turned on at full blast. My super sensitivity—the thing that had caused me so much pain as Little Megan—became my superpower. I began using my empathy and sensitivity to channel for my clients and help them write copy and marketing content that made people say, "You read my mind!" Together we were changing the marketing paradigm, and watching an industry built on manipulation and twisting words become a place for honest connection. I showed my clients how to write content that healed others and also healed them because they were finally able to speak their truths, write from their hearts, and share their big gifts in clear, compelling ways.

I stopped fearing that connection would lead to rejection. I made openness my trademark. Now I smile when people tell me they admire how vulnerable I am in my writing. I stopped myself from being vulnerable for so long because it didn't feel safe. But it's what my soul came in wanting from the beginning: *Just let me be who I am and let me be loved for that.*

Ultimately, I realized that simply because I wasn't meant to be a mother of humans, it didn't mean I wasn't a nourishing presence. I am the mother of words, birthing ideas, and bringing a new age to light.

* * *

YOU BET your bottom dollar I still get activated. I still have an over-coupling that tells my Radiance to fire up when I'm anxious, scared, upset, or disturbed, but I also have tools to stay present in my body. To experience safety. To titrate. To examine the feelings. To write them out. Cry them out. Dance them out. To ask for help from my love, who sees and accepts all of me. Just as I accept all of myself.

Now, I shine my light more and more. I embrace being a writer. I've written and published five books, four of them about writing. As I write this, I'm midway through creating a writing oracle deck, which combines wisdom from my writing coaching practice and deep whisperings from my soul.

Whereas I used to cower behind rational thought, now, I both reveal and revel in my intuitive gifts. I share my spiritual journey. I hold my frequency so strongly and so cleanly that I can hold space for other highly-sensitive empaths and channels. They tell me that I provide for them what they're used to providing for others. That feels so beautiful. Not only am I safe in myself, but I also invite others to be safe in themselves. All because I broke the silence.

* * *

GOODBYE, shame. Goodbye, silence. Thank you. I love you. I'm sorry. I forgive you.

ABOUT THE AUTHOR

MEGAN BARNHARD

Megan Barnhard is a Story Magician and an intuitive writing coach for visionary leaders. She helps coaches, healers, and guides wrap their gifts in words and unleash the bold messages in their hearts. Megan believes that writing is everyone's birthright, and she's committed to helping people find their Wise Writer Within and write in flow. With her coaching, books, and retreats, Megan's on a mission to help writers heal themselves and the world through storytelling. She is also an author who delights in sharing her own journey and leading with playful vulnerability. Megan lives with her husband and their two clever black cats.

Learn more and connect here:

https://www.facebook.com/megan.barnhard.writer

https://www.facebook.com/groups/writeinflow

https://www.instagram.com/writewithmegan

https://www.meganbarnhard.com

MELISSA CHERNOW

THE SOUND OF HONEY

"I have something for you girls."

We had barely walked into her house, and my grandmother was already showering us with love, adoration, and gifts. My sister and I each opened a pair of aqua blue shorts. They had an elastic waistband and were covered with the brightest flowers—oranges, greens, and pinks. I didn't care that they were a few sizes too big; I was elated and wrapped my six year old arms around my Grandma Belle in gratitude.

After exchanging smiles and excitement, she then whispered that she had another surprise for us. She brought my sister and I into her den (my parents stayed in the main room) and emerged from the closet with two full-sized Hershey's chocolate bars. My smile must have been as big as the candy.

"Don't tell your parents." She grinned. It felt like the most fun secret, and I was overjoyed to be its keeper, chocolate in hand.

Four years later, my sister and I were getting ready for our first dance class. I asked my mom what we should wear, and she encouraged us to choose something comfortable and easy to move around in. I excitedly reached for my bright floral shorts—they finally fit. My sister wore hers too.

When we arrived at the studio, we completed the necessary paperwork for class since this was our first time. By the time we entered the studio, everyone was already seated and listening to the teacher. My sister and I stepped closer as the instructor introduced us to the class, but I stopped listening when I saw two of the girls start laughing and snickering.

Confusion turned to embarrassment when I realized why they were laughing at us. Everyone else was wearing all black, some version of a black leotard with black tights or a black t-shirt with black leggings—the uniform.

I was gutted. My heart broke into a million pieces, and I never wanted to wear those stupid shorts ever again. I mean, Who even wears bright patterned shorts like that?

When we got home from class, I immediately changed my clothes and shoved those shorts to the back of my closet on the very bottom shelf. I was never going to wear them again. I was mad and confused. If dance is about expression, Why was everyone in the same plain outfit?

* * *

Several months later, my mom took me to get my first ever manicure. It was all I wanted for my birthday. She indulged me (I think somewhat reluctantly), and I couldn't contain my excitement. I wanted the brightest, prettiest coral I could find. It was my favorite color, and I thought it would look nice against my sun-kissed summer skin.

I stood in front of the rows and rows of polishes, first browsing the colors at my eye level—purples, deep reds, a few blues and greens. I stretched my neck up to the next row. I saw some bright oranges and eventually the corals. I looked higher and higher and found a full row of classic reds, and above those, more rows of neutral polishes than I could count. I wondered why someone would want to paint their nails neutral. It was a curious but rather quick thought as I returned my gaze to the coral section. I selected my favorite shade and turned to my mom with a smile.

The nail technicians seated me a few minutes later, my feet swinging back and forth with joy. I looked to the other ladies getting their nails done, and all I saw were bottles of neutral polish—neutral with a touch of mauve, neutral with a touch of pink, neutral, and more neutral. I was perplexed.

I glanced back at the vibrant peachy pink paint coloring my nails and smiled. Then came the little shoulder massage while my nails were drying. As if I hadn't already been sold on this experience. This was the best day ever, the best birthday ever!

It can be said that the paradox of age is that when you're young, you want to be a grown-up, but as you age, all you want to be is a kid again.

I now see that when I reached an age of wanting to be "grown-up" and "mature," it largely stemmed from the desire to fit in. In community that doesn't celebrate individual expression, conformity reigns. Something as simple as seeing everyone around you choose the same nail color can impact your creative essence.

By the time high school rolled around, I had started wearing more black. When I got my nails done, I chose pinky neutral tones, especially when I started internships in college. Sure, they looked sophisticated and matched every outfit, but everything matched when you wore all black.

I consciously noticed I was using my visual self-expression to not stand out. What I didn't realize was that I had also unconsciously attempted to fly under the radar with my verbal self-expression too. This revealed itself more subtly.

* * *

IT STARTS AS WHISPERS. They're almost too easy to ignore. Then the whispers become louder commentary which gets set ablaze if not given attention. Thank goodness for that. Thank goodness my body started yelling. For over twenty years, I wasn't listening to the whispers.

The whispers turned to screams in March 2020, at the beginning of the coronavirus pandemic in the United States. My stomach pains, loss of appetite, and fatigue arrived every month. They synced with my menstrual cycle, but not in the way you might expect.

I had just learned about the four phases of the menstrual cycle (which needs to be taught in school). I took particular interest in the ovulatory phase, as it's known to be a time of higher energy. When you apply that information to business, it can be a great time for program or product launches, live masterclasses, or pretty much anything forward facing. I ran with that information and planned my next coaching program launch to coincide with my ovulatory phase.

It flopped. Well, I can't even say it flopped, because it didn't even happen. Why? Those mystery pains and exhaustion emerged, and I was out for five days.

Okay, let's try again next month, I thought.

In April, the mystery illness returned. Then, the same story in May. And June. Yep, then in July too. Like clockwork. Its arrival, duration, and symptoms were identical every month. I was frustrated. I was curious. And, I was mad at my body.

One look at my human design chart shows that I'm a problem solver by nature. I had months of data and personal experience to assess now. I was determined to get to the bottom of this.

While listening to Maroon 5's, "She Will Be Loved" (one of my all-time top three favorite songs), it clicked. It's funny how the songs and movies we loved growing up, a lot of the time, touch on our desires. I wanted to be loved for my fullness, my bigness, my "weirdness"—for me. But I'd learned from a young age that my expression wasn't welcome. This was mostly my verbal expression. This is what I meant earlier when I said I tried to fly under the radar with my verbal self-expression. In other words, I learned it was safer to be quiet and unnoticed.

I was praised for being easygoing, which really meant I was praised for not sharing my opinion and agreeing with everyone else's.

I was told my emotions were too much, so I learned to keep them to myself.

I observed that hard conversations were either avoided or blown way out of proportion.

I became scared to use my voice: any time I did, I was rejected or ignored. My body had been taking notes, carefully recording what was safe and what was not. Which takes us back to my epiphany about that mystery cyclical illness: My body was protecting me. I was scared of being seen, terrified, actually.

The years and years of biting my tongue and censoring my expression in an attempt to not be rejected or ignored now screamed at me. At any attempt to be more visible or share my authentic voice, my body stopped me. The mystery illness cycle was no longer a mystery: it was a protection mechanism just like the black clothes disguised as chic and the plain nails that essentially went unnoticed.

Upon connecting the dots with such clarity, I apologized to my body and thanked her for protecting me. She was doing what she thought was best. This apology is ongoing as I continue to heal.

I was excited to take this information to the somatic leadership coach I had just started working with, eager to resolve the root of this. I received so much more than that. The nervous system work we began doing was the most honest, meaningful, and effective healing I had ever done. I still don't have the right words to capture how profound the process is, but in the simplest terms, it's a body-based approach to healing. The body keeps score, and I was discovering the depth of this truth on a whole new level. WIthin three months, we resolved the stomach issues because we tended to the root of the issue. We addressed the beliefs around visibility that my body had been carrying rather than dousing my body in visibility strategies or medical testing that would never actually help given the root of the issue.

Another interesting conversation was happening at this time.

"I think you're a good candidate for jaw surgery." My jaw dropped (albeit crookedly) upon hearing those words. I knew my pain was real and constant, but I never would have suspected it warranted surgery. I could appreciate my dentist's professional opinion; I mean the MRI images staring back at me made it obvious, but as he told me about the surgery, the different approaches we could take, and what postoperative physical therapy would look like, my body whispered, *no.* I wasn't going to ignore it. I knew in my heart of hearts, that the root of the problem wasn't purely structural, it was emotional too.

Years of people-pleasing were catching up with me physically. Before walking out of the dentist's office, I promised myself I would start using my voice more, then revisit the idea of surgery down the line if necessary. To me, jaw surgery would have been a Band-Aid to a deeper issue. It might have provided temporary or partial relief, but it wouldn't resolve the issue sustainably or entirely if I didn't also start using my voice. I wanted to start there. I wanted to start using my voice. That desire itself was huge for me.

My vow to use my voice meant a lot of things I was uncomfortable with, things I wasn't used to. It meant saying no. It meant offering my ideas and opinions at the (to my nervous system and inner children, very scary,) risk of rejection. It meant getting comfortable with being an outsider and paving my own path, even when nobody understood me. It meant sharing my opinion, even (and especially) when it was contrary to the group, not to ruffle their feathers, but to respect mine.

My body was terrified. It's not like I could jump off the diving board into the deep end. This fear ran deep to the early ages of childhood. So, like a child learning to swim, I strapped floaties around my arms and took the first step into the pool (in the shallow end of course). I chose the relationships I felt the most reciprocity in and started sharing more of my voice. A lot of it seemed silly, saying no to the simplest of things, but my body was grateful every time. I was using my body as my guide. Even though my heart would race, my body felt alive and free after every share, no matter the subject. This began an entirely new, much kinder relationship with my body.

Instead of my mind and past pains running the show, I let my body lead the way. We were a team. We said no to social invitations and family dinners. We said no to fun trips and plans with friends. These no's felt excruciating to my mind, but they felt liberating to my body like I could finally breathe. I was learning to swim.

Any sustainable process of unlearning takes time, so what helped me most during that time was looking to compound interest: I viewed every small action as a huge win and appreciated their cumulative effect, knowing this was the foundation from which I was finding my freedom.

* * *

I SUSPECT my thyroid issues started silently emerging at the beginning of the pandemic as well. Aside from that mystery illness cycle that started in March 2020, I wasn't feeling myself. This was why the ovulatory phase and projected energy were so intriguing to me during that phase.

The doctor ran bloodwork, which always came back in-range. After a year of in-range labs, I started doing my own research and learned about functional medicine. Thank goodness I did. I learned that in-range doesn't necessarily mean ideal. Functional ranges show what's optimal to function. Functional ranges for my bloodwork revealed my thyroid numbers were off. Further testing, almost a year after that, showed thyroid antibodies: I have Hashimoto's thyroiditis, an autoimmune disease of the thyroid. I didn't take this as a diagnosis. I saw it as valuable information on my healing journey. It led me to learn about which foods, exercises, supplements, and activities could support my body, as well as the things that could contribute to my symptoms.

The voice of my body was speaking clearly, and I was finally listening and finally supporting it.

It took time, yet it was simple.

Looking at it now, it all makes sense.

I'd been clenching my teeth since seventh grade. My TMJ (temporomandibular joint dysfunction) had become so advanced over the years, that the pain crawled down my spine and radiated into my shoulder. Every yawn was a symphony of jaw pops, cracks, and clicks.

My body was literally showing me where I was emotionally hurting and energetically restricting myself. Every symptom that arose directly related to the throat chakra: our energy center for communication and expression.

When I take a step back and look at the purpose of it all, I see the whispers as the greatest setup for me to finally choose my natural expression. The etymology of my name agrees: Melissa means honey or honeybee in Greek. The natural remedy for a sore throat is a spoonful of local honey. It's sweet, warm, and golden. Soothing and naturally healing. It has staying power and gives life. I feel most myself when I access these qualities energetically within my body when I speak.

I call it the sound of honey: *speak with the sound of honey.*

When a critical voice in my head emerges, I meet it with the sound of honey, kind and compassionate.

When having hard conversations, I meet it with the sound of honey, my cue to access the softness, strength, and sweetness that's our core essence from the moment we're born.

When the rigidity and fast pace of fear-based thinking gets loud, I meet it with the sound of honey, slow, smooth, and grounded.

When my body whispers or I want anything but neutral on my nails, or when my inner child wants to pick out my outfit for the day, I respond with the sound of honey, with warmth and kindness.

I speak with the sound of honey to myself, my body, my community, my dreams, and my ideas. It's a much kinder ecosystem than the one the world prescribes. It's far more natural and harmonious. It feels like home. Of course our healing would be our homecoming.

When the world tries to keep you silenced, meet it with the sound of honey.

ABOUT THE AUTHOR

MELISSA CHERNOW

Melissa Chernow is a voice and visibility coach, author, and founder of Cardinal Publishing House. She works with leaders to feel safe in their bodies, so they can speak from the heart with confidence and clarity. Her publishing house creates impact-driven books that reveal the many textures of humanity while inspiring authors and readers alike to live more authentically, joyfully, and within their soul's integrity.

Learn more and connect here:

cardinalpublishinghouse@gmail.com

www.instagram.com/melissamelrose_

www.melissachernow.com

MICHELLE L. GUGELMEYER

THE REFORMATIONS OF A PEOPLE-PLEASER

I remember the beginning of my life vividly. I was an extremely active child, and I was given space to explore and expel energy. Living in a rural location, just steps away from a little tributary off the Rock River in Illinois, I studied the forest and the riverbank. I picked wildflowers and raspberries, sang and danced in the dappled sunshine, communed with fauna, and mimicked bird calls. I hunted for stones, skipping the flat, smooth ones across the river's surface. I examined the habits of bees and other pollinators, never once experiencing the harsh poke of a stinger. The forest enveloped me and welcomed me as if I were born there. All I had to do was yell to Dad that I was leaving and off I would go. When I would hear Dad's whistle to signal me home, it was a sign that I may have lingered too long. I knew the feeling of joy nearly every day. I knew it was my birthright.

My connection to nature has run deep since those beginnings. It was on those riverbanks that I found my intuitive channel to the ethereal realm. I was reverent for the beings who walked the forest before me. I felt the memories and heard the whispers of the indigenous people who had lived along those same banks. There were some parts of the forest that whispered I shouldn't venture further. I knew it was a warning of some kind and I listened. Freedom and joy permeated every cell of my body when I was alone in the forest and that became the roots of my future resilience.

Mom, and her career aspirations, came first and if I could get out of the house for a while, she was thankful. Dad, however, often took me on adventures through the woodland and junkyards. He loved my adventurous heart. In my forest wonderland I was at liberty to be my authentic self. At school, I was too spirited for the adults around me.

Kindergarten was when I started to realize I wasn't like the other kids. I couldn't sit still in my seat. Today, there would probably be letters to label me and a pill to keep me calm. If the teacher left the room, I was up and wandering. My intention was to explore and connect with others; the result was I spent a lot of time with my nose in a corner. Freedom wasn't allowed there.

When I was eight, my brother was born, much to the surprise of my parents. This is when a patriarchal structure began to be set between my brother and me. I felt that the sun rose and set on his ass. Mom adored him. He was one year old when I tossed one of his toys out of my room, and Mom beat me with a belt.

As we grew, I had to forgo extracurricular activities at school to be his nanny. I was forced to help Mom clean his room, as well as do the other chores I had around the house. She would wake me up at eight in the morning on weekends to clean the house. She was a smoker, so once a month I would have to wash the nicotine off the walls. I did not see fairness between the responsibilities that were given to me and those given to my brother. My freedom was drastically reduced after his birth.

Mom was a business superstar. She was one of those women who fought hard to hold positions that, previously, only men had been afforded. This was her mission. I saw her caught between blazing a trail for women and being stuck in the people-pleasing rigidity of the fifties housewife. She essentially used me as her right hand. I felt like my hopes and dreams for my future were never a consideration. I don't remember a time when we discussed what I wanted to be when I grew up. In fact, she wasn't supportive when I went to college. I realized then that her life of competing with men in the workplace had bled into her competing with me. She didn't want my future successes to eclipse hers.

During adolescence, I began a phase of people-pleasing that was rooted in being an overachiever at school and at my after-school job, where I was quickly promoted to shift supervisor. It turns out the people-pleasing standards needed for Mom were stellar when used in the workplace. I misconstrued this people-please as work ethic.

My teenage years unearthed a rebellion. I started dressing like Robert Smith from The Cure and hung around other people who dressed similarly. My friends had mohawks, punky clothes, and attitudes. Some might call this goth. I started to lean into music and art, much of which was shocking to my mother. When I was fourteen, she gifted me a makeup pallet. When I used it, she said I looked like a clown (It was the eighties. We all looked like clowns). I had learned fashion and personal style were a means of creative expression and a way to assuage feelings of resentment. Around this same time, I was gifted a deck of tarot cards. I would soon discover how pivotal this was for me. Like the makeup pallet there was an air of rebellion around them. In the years to follow I would learn that this tool would be pivotal as a direct conduit to the divine, validating the nudges I had received throughout my life. The tarot would also become a clear teacher about having boundaries.

Days after my eighteenth birthday I had an awakening about personal boundaries. About a month before I graduated from high school, I came home after curfew, and my parents were sitting on the sofa, waiting for me. As I was reprimanded for being late, I firmly stated that I was now an adult; I would no longer be adhering to a curfew. I remember their shocked faces, but they didn't disagree with me. I was standing in my power.

I was more than ready to handle this freedom. This was the first time I consciously realized I had followed a nudge from within. I enrolled in community college (with no help from my parents), got a new job, and felt powerful. I majored in art, much to Mother's disappointment. I was confused that suddenly she was taking an interest. I changed my major to business after being told art was not profitable. I was resentful of this for years.

The rebellion of listening to my intuition and creating better boundaries was what I needed for self-empowerment. I learned that self-empowerment was an abundant vibration. To stay in that vibration, I needed self-awareness skills. At this point in my life, those skills were underdeveloped.

As I shifted into adulthood, a new opportunity to people-please presented itself; I met the boyfriend who would become my husband.

We met in my second year of college; he was my first serious boyfriend. I was in love. I know now this was a trauma bond. We were inseparable. He was oppressive. I couldn't go anywhere without him, except work or home. I was blind to the oppression. I felt loved and adored. The parts of me that felt ignored and troublesome were welcomed by him.

However, it would soon become clear that his insecurity ran deep. I was constantly having to deflect my boyfriend's feelings of jealousy. The model I had been shown was to stay together and to work through hard times. It was clear my parents didn't like him, and our partnership would not be supported. I left home, and I didn't speak to my family for nearly a year. During my year of silence, I married him.

Now married, the patriarchal structure began to confine me again. It was almost immediate. My husband belittled me for "trying to wear the pants." His attempts to control me were met with my need to impose expectations on him. I would have left the marriage, but I knew there was a human being in the ether waiting for me. I knew that I had a biological link to this man because of the child that was seeking me. I had seen images in my dreams of the two of us as parents, so I stuck it out. I often wonder what life may have been like if it didn't. After a short time, my reality became that I was married to an addict.

Again, I was imprisoned. I tried micromanaging my husband into sobriety—it failed. He would slip in and out of sobriety. There would be long stretches when he would be sober, and life was amazing. When he was using, catastrophes would happen regularly. All the decisions I made were related to getting him healthy so I could move on with the things I wanted to do in life. Destiny was calling to me to follow my life's purpose, yet I was not listening. I was people-pleasing to him and honoring the institution of marriage.

In 1999, after being married for six years, I became pregnant. This is when I made a commitment to myself to listen to my intuition unequivocally. I was adamant about having a home birth. I was able to stand in my power differently. My boundaries were being respected. My boundaries were my authenticity. Listening to my intuition would still be a challenge and I would slip into relapses of people pleasing again and again in the years to come.

Being pregnant and housing this powerful soul in my womb would change the course of my life forever. I was empowered. I was imposing boundaries and structure. I was taking back my power. My husband saw this and was in awe. He began to show a less argumentative, oppressive side. He was truly supportive and an active teammate. I will always be grateful for his sobriety during those years. I felt like I had a partner. I started using my tarot cards again. I chose to use alternative care providers throughout my pregnancy opting to forgo allopathic interventions. I chose practitioners that provided chiropractic, massage, yoga, and pranayama (breathwork) services. My intuition led me exactly where I needed to go every time. It became the source in my life I trusted the most.

My husband and I made an appointment at a birth center and met with a nurse-midwife. I didn't feel it was the right fit. But as I stopped at a local health food store following up on her recommendation of chewable papaya for my heartburn, I happened upon an advertisement for a homebirth midwife group. The breadcrumb trail that appeared was a gift from following the nudges. I hired the homebirth midwife group and went on to have a beautiful homebirth. The photos from our birthing experience would later be showcased as a full page spread in the Midwifery Today publication.

I had an immediate psychic bond with my unborn baby. My intuition told me the baby was female. After a few months, I knew her name was Grace. There were times during my pregnancy that I saw glimpses in my mind's eye of raising her alone. It became my biggest fear. Months after our perfect, life-changing home waterbirth, where my husband and I worked in harmony with our midwife, I started to see evidence of my impending future. My biggest fear did, in fact, become a reality. With all my attention being used to care for a newborn, my husband felt slighted and relapsed into his self-destructive patterns. Eleven and a half traumatic years later, at the age of forty, he died from an overdose.

For the first part of my child's life, my experience as a care-giver served her well. I tended to her needs readily. I breastfed her until she was almost three. We took hikes through the forest. I experimented with babywearing methods. I got involved with La Leche League and settled into a community of like-minded moms. I loved every aspect of motherhood. I started seeing a wonderful therapist and shaman. I finally understood that people-pleasing was manipulation and that it comes from a place of fear, not love. I learned this pattern stemmed from the conditioning modeled for me by my parents and other caregivers. I was taught to be ready for anything that could go wrong. It was during this time of my life that I started taking ownership of my fate. I was entering what my daughter would later deem "the hippy years." I had incorrectly learned that pathologically doing things to meet the needs of others at my own expense didn't serve anyone. It was most likely that the people I engaged with felt my lack of authenticity.

When it was time for her to attend school, I was involved with her class. Yet, it was soon obvious public school (another patriarchal structure) was not working for her. Bullying by both male students and teachers became a huge problem. Even with all my time spent at the school and listening to staff, it was clear they were not going to support my daughter the way she needed.

We decided to homeschool at the beginning of her third-grade year, and I leaned into the adjustment. I saw how Grace needed freedom, just like I did. As she grew into her teen years, I saw Grace beginning the people-pleasing patterns in her relationships that she had witnessed between myself and her father. She was changing and we weren't communicating like we had when she was little. She went through a period of depression, in which she stopped eating. Later, I found out that she had been assaulted during this time. The period after the death of my husband and her father was one of the lowest times in our lives.

One day, when she was closer to adulthood, she told me she felt like I was manipulative. I was startled, and I needed to take time to process what she meant. After processing, I realized I had fallen into the people-pleasing pattern, again. When we would have discussions (argue) I would never state how I truly felt. I tried at all costs to avoid conflict or rocking the boat. I would agree to things to avoid discomfort, and then later felt resentful, which confused her. I also found myself minimizing her emotions. Something that had been done to me as a kid. I thought by keeping my true opinions to myself and allowing her freedom she would have fewer issues with me and, in turn, life would be peaceful. I needed a more refined approach to my parenting. I was parenting in a way that had not been modeled for me and I was doing it alone. I realized that being her mom was teaching me so much. And, how much I needed to say exactly what I meant. I needed to put my own needs first so I could act with clarity and so we could pursue things that were important to both of us. People-pleasing in my parenting came from a desire to be in control because I felt powerless.

During our years of homeschooling, I built a successful massage therapy practice and cultivated a following as a yoga instructor and empowerment coach. This took me on a new journey of deep self-healing.

As Grace grew into an adult and freedom began to stalk me, I found myself in a dark spot. My purpose had revolved around my family my entire life. I sought support from other healers and guides. I stepped out of my comfort zone and tried new career paths, but nothing felt aligned. I was still people-pleasing by keeping my greatest gift, my connection to my intuition, a secret. I even became licensed to sell insurance in multiple states only to feel unaligned because of the shadiness of the company I worked for. Finally, I hired a series of coaches who were able to get me turned in the right direction. It was with their support that I was able to package my skills and begin a new business. I had been giving intuitive readings and tarot card readings as a side hustle since Grace's birth. Suddenly, I was the closest to my life's purpose than ever before and I stepped into a place of visibility. I came out of the spiritual closet. I was finally living in my authenticity.

Now, I coach others on how to find their empowerment and live through their truth. I guide them as they discover their purpose and show them techniques for tapping into intuition. I hold space for them to discover the areas that need to shift. We create a plan together on how to lift from dense vibrations. I hold space for and assist as they move in and out of their own relapses. I have learned that being in an elevated frequency is the most abundant way to live. I am now strategic in terms of self-awareness. I know sustainability means I need support. There is value in obtaining support. Healing is a dance; back and forth. There is no linear path through grief. Life is the ouroboros, wrapping around itself. Sometimes, we are in flow, we ascend to new heights, and then something shitty emerges. We take pause, get curious, delve, and forgive. The delving isn't glamorous, but grit makes the pearl. It takes awareness, dedication to self, and finding the exact right brand of support. Did I mention forgiveness? Let me mention it again. Forgiveness also needs a chapter of its own.

I still see people-pleasing patterns pop up. Like when I allow a friend to coerce me into meeting up when my schedule is full, and I really need time for myself; the resistance to reschedule because I don't want to disappoint. Or, when I'm not being authentic about a topic because I don't want to take the time to communicate how I really feel; it is a choice to speak and act with authenticity consistently. When good boundaries are set, unapologetically, self-empowerment is born, and a connection is made. Using the voice to communicate boundaries is healing. If something doesn't feel right, it's not. Shrinking to fit someone else's needs is toxic.

Walking my purpose-driven path is my birthright. My path is home. Home is where my heart lives. I love me. I forgive myself for people-pleasing. I forgive my mother for repeating patterns that were modeled for her. My hope is that in healing these parts of myself, I am an impetus of healing for the lineage of all the divine feminine energy connected to me. I hope the people-pleaser in you feels this, forgives, and steps into the beautiful light of your authenticity.

ABOUT THE AUTHOR

MICHELLE L. GUGELMEYER

Michelle Gugelmeyer is a spiritual leader, multi-dimensional healer, artist, and entrepreneur. Her mission is to provide support and empowerment to individuals as they break free from old patterns, stagnation and are ready for innovation and leaving their comfort zone. Michelle enjoys many avenues of creative expression. Her favorite ways to spend her time involve being with family, working in her flower beds, picking veggies in the garden, exploring, traveling the world and experiencing different cultures. Michelle considers herself a lifelong student of life's mysteries. She lives and works from her home in the upper Mississippi River Valley in northwestern Illinois with her daughter, Grace, a college student, their tortie cat, Eve, and their Caique parrot, Bubs. She works as an intuitive business strategist, transformational coach, and psychic-medium serving souls across the globe.

Learn more and connect here:

Gugelmeyer Holistic Coaching and Consulting

gugelmeyercoaching@gmail.com

https://www.facebook.com/MichelleGugelmeyerIntuitiveBusinessStrategist

https://michellegugelmeyerholisticcoaching.lpages.co/transform-with-tarot

ROXY SEWELL

LUNA: A JOURNEY OF HEALING INTO MOTHERHOOD

"The English language lacks the words to mourn an absence. For the loss of a parent, grandparent, spouse, child, or friend, we have all manner of words and phrases, some helpful some not. Still, we are conditioned to say something, even if it is only 'I'm sorry for your loss." But for an absence, for someone who was never there at all, we are wordless to capture that particular emptiness. For those who deeply want children and are denied them, those missing babies hover like silent ephemeral shadows over their lives. Who can describe the feel of a tiny hand that is never held?" - Anonymous

There is a person in my life that most people are unaware of; she exists, not on this earth, but rather in the beating heart of my dreams. Dreams that have been coming to me since 2018 when I was living in Washington DC. The first night I met her was when I was thirty-one years old. I was asleep in my bed which sat comfortably on the eighteenth floor of my high-rise apartment. My boyfriend, Sean (now my husband), was sleeping next to me and our two cats were purring at our feet. We were the happiest family; small yet full of love.

In my dream, I was walking alone through a field of flowers. Out of the blue, a barefoot little girl in a white linen dress came skipping toward me. Her arms were outstretched making sure that each finger touched its own flower. Her smile was magnetic, and her body held a light that covered the space around her in rainbow fractals. I could not help but smile when I saw her and, intuitively, I knew she was mine to know. Once she reached me, she stopped, looked up at me with her ocean-green eyes, tugged at my dress, and in a voice that sounded like a chorus of soft bells, she spoke. Her voice was ethereal, "Mom! Don't you know my name? My name is Luna! Mommy! My name is Luna." Her words were full of sass and sprinkled with what I could only label as a slight annoyance.

Before I could say a single word, I woke up. I opened my eyes and gasped for air. I sat up in my bed, turned to Sean, and woke him up with an urgency that felt as if a fire had been lit inside my womb.

"Her name is Luna!"

Sean just stared at me, confusion covering every ounce of his still-sleeping face.

"Our daughter, her name is Luna. I saw her in my dream; she is so beautiful!" Then, I began to cry. I loved her so much already.

When I first met Luna, I was filled with an excitement so pure. An excitement that held the innocence of a maiden who had no idea of the grief that awaited her. Everything changed for my little family that night. My dream was surreal; it was as vivid as any lived experience. It evoked each of my senses and created a space deep within my heart that could only be inhabited by her. In every way possible, Luna unveiled everything I didn't know I wanted, as well as everything I didn't know I needed. She came to change me, to bring me home to her, and, also, to bring me home to myself.

My dream of Luna came during a liminal phase of my life—a phase in which I was struggling to allow myself to move forward in my own love story. Although I was madly in love with Sean and I wanted to spend the rest of my life with him, I had no desire to be married. I had been married once before in my twenties, and the experience left a traumatically sour taste in my mouth. I didn't trust it. More specifically, I didn't trust myself in it. Marriage, as I saw it, was a giant recipe for heartache and divorce. And so, for me, happiness looked like this —a simple love with my best friend, the two of us choosing to do life next to one another, and our two cats acting as our children. In my eyes, Sean and I were already a family. Marriage be damned.

At this time, my ability to see myself as a mother was also non-existent. Not because I did not want to be a mother, on the contrary, I wanted nothing more. But rather, it was because I was afraid to change any vital part of my existence. My liminal phase was all about creating a chamber of unchanged stillness. I could accept transient physical changes such as moving cities, traveling, or even changing jobs, but when it came to changing my relationship or my family, I was unwilling to budge. Change was unreliable. It held the power of duality in its hands. It could expand my life in joy as easily as it could take it all away. It could do this in just one breath. And so, I stayed still. I refused to change, refused to move forward, and refused to expand.

It's funny how life works. We can resist change, yet we are promised nothing but it. Time moves us forward in a spiral motion. Just like the moon itself, we move round and round, changing, evolving, and expanding. Our souls know the path we are meant to take long before our human self can begin to comprehend it; surrendering to this unknowing is our sacred journey. This is our healing.

All of us are here to heal, to show ourselves that it is safe to open and expand our hearts, that it is safe to come out of hiding and share our voices, to make life one altar, one ritual, and one moving prayer. Luna came into my life unexpectedly at just the right time. She forced me out of my liminal phase and out of my cocoon. She urged me to move forward into my new life, and in doing so, I began to dream new dreams. I began to heal in deeper ways. Ever so slowly, I began to trust myself to love again, and, more importantly, I began to trust myself to be loved again. This trust expanded my soul in such a way that on June 8, 2019, in a little garden by the beach, Sean and I became husband and wife.

Luna would continue to appear to me for years. Night after night I would enter a parallel universe in which my daughter was very much alive. The more I dreamt of her, the clearer she became. Morning after morning, I would wake up and tell Sean all about our little girl. I filled my journals with letters to her and began to seek her out through my meditations as well. Each time she appeared to me I felt as if she was bringing me closer to her, showing me an undiscovered part of her soul that was longing to be seen. I heard her laugh and so did Sean as she began to appear in his dreams too. I felt her mischievous nature. I held her in my arms. I sang her lullabies that I had written just for her. I was, in every way possible, becoming her mother.

Luna's clear and persistent presence made it feel as if she were a single breath away, that all we needed to do was tell her it was time and she would appear in my womb, ready to be birthed like magic. It felt easy—too easy. I relished in the simplicity of it all.

And so, in January of 2020, we began to try to conceive.

When Sean and I first began trying to conceive, the experience was filled with cosmic-sized optimism. We radiated joy. We were explorers heading out into the frontier of parenthood. We felt as if we could see the horizon, touch the next chapter of our life, and land in the enchanting phase of motherhood and fatherhood with an ease that came as easy as breathing. With our excitement tightly wrapped in the most precious of ways, we began to prepare for the arrival of our little moon. We knew that she was just around the corner.

Month after month we waited like children on the eve of Christmas.

Month after month we waited...and waited...and waited.

And yet, no Luna. Instead, we were greeted with monthly cycles of blood. My ever-so-reliable womb bleeding like clockwork, never a day late.

After six months of trying to conceive, our optimism began to shift. Worry had begun to dilute our enthusiasm as grief began to creep into our lives. Six months turned into one year, and it was then that we received our official diagnosis: unexplained infertility. Today, I am writing this chapter over two and a half years into our journey.

There is a grief that is unique to infertility. A grief that opens your heart in two and creates a space deep within yourself that only you can inhabit. This space resembles a birth canal, a birth canal that never seems to quite open. As a result, you are left waiting in a cold silence that is seemingly endless. The grief of infertility is unique in that you yearn for someone you have never met. You ache to hold the tiny hands of a child that has never been born. The more time that passes, the deeper and more painful this yearning becomes until, eventually, you are left with a pain so deep that your heart expands to the point of nearly breaking.

I owe a deep gratitude to grief. In my mind, she appears as a primordial mother that resembles the goddesses of ancient mythology. She comes to me draped in truth with arms outstretched and a smile so gentle, yet also, strong in its all-knowing. She calls me forward and welcomes my tears, honoring the depth of my sorrow, and celebrating her total existence with me. My grief-mother takes me on a journey, a journey deep inside of myself, that will somehow show me the range of my full capacity to love, witness, and be held. These journeys have proven to be life-changing as they have allowed my voice to express the full range of my emotions. They have allowed my tears to sing what my voice has yet to create words for.

As women, we are told to hide our grief. To silence our wounds that lay deep within our wombs. But the deeper I grieved for Luna, the louder my wounds became. Until eventually, they began to call me inward, inward toward my pain.

* * *

I LONGED FOR LUNA, and I began to search for her everywhere. I looked for her in my dreams, in my meditations, and through my rituals. I looked for her in nature, in the butterflies that flew in my backyard, and in the flowers that bloomed overnight. I looked for her in the landscapes, in the deserts out west, in the oceans down south, in the trees of the mighty Sequoia National Forest, and in the snow-filled hiking trails of Mount Rainier. Everywhere I went and in every hidden piece of magic I found, I looked for her and saw her there.

And, while all those places allowed me to see her in my own way, it was the moon that brought me closest to her.

To most, the moon is just the moon, an object hanging in the sky. But to me, the moon is and has always been so much more. When I look up at the moon I hear promises, laughter, and the pitter-patter of feet running across the floor and kicking a ball with delight. When I look up at the moon I see motherhood, hope, and grief all tied into one. The moon promises nothing but change. It promises grief and love as a whole experience. Perhaps, this is why she is named Luna. Because, perhaps, for me, it wasn't supposed to be easy. Perhaps, I was supposed to learn to love her through the depth of my own grief.

Night after night, I would sit under the moon writing in my journal while moving in ritual, searching for answers—searching for her. Silence became my companion in grief. In my silence, I heard the voice of the moon speaking to me from the other side of time. I heard her voice rising as it vibrated from the depth of my womb all the way up to the crown of my head. Night after night, I would hear her giggling voice whispering to me, "I am here momma. Trust me, I am here. Look for me not in the sky, not 'out there,' but rather in the depth of your womb. I am here waiting for you."

For centuries women have been taught to detach from our wombs. But the womb is a portal for deep connection. It is our doorway, our threshold into the unknown. It initiates us into the lunar mysteries of death and rebirth and of maiden-mother-crone. It is a space where alchemy happens, where love and hope meet pain and shame. The stories of my unsilencing are ever so delicately woven in with my stories of shame. Understanding where I held these stories in my body, where they came from, how they influenced my life, and how I used them as weapons of self-destruction has allowed me to begin to release them one by one as alchemical offerings. By journeying inward towards my shame with such reverence, I held space for myself to be imperfect. I allowed myself to hold those imperfections without denial and in compassionate truth. In doing so, I became my own moving ritual, releasing myself from the chains of silence placed around my throat centuries ago. The more I loosened these chains, the deeper I moved into my body and womb space. The deeper I moved into my womb, the more I began to heal. It is from my womb that my voice grows.

One cold January night under the light of the full moon, I wrote a letter to my womb asking her to show me the depth of my hidden truth. I wrote and wrote, allowing my pen to move without the judgment of my mind and, in doing so, I felt my shame step forward, shame that had been hiding in the silent crevices of my womb.

The shame of my infertility was not new to my body. It began to build itself deep within my womb many years before the phrase, "You have unexplained infertility" was ever spoken to me. Throughout the entirety of my life, my womb was a space that held all my deepest secrets and all of my truth. She held my inner fire which paved the way for my successful career. She held the intimacy of each of my past love stories and the passion behind their varied breakups. She held the sacredness from that most intimate night in which my husband and I became more than just best friends. She held Luna. She knew her story. She held our prayer.

My womb held the most precious parts of me. She wrapped them in a ribbon of joy. She did this while also holding the parts of me that were darker and less pretty. The parts that I had wrapped in shame like my own scarlet letters: shame from the sexual abuse in my past, personal regrets where friendships were lost, mistakes I made in my career, and wild nights filled with both fun and regret. My womb held it all.

The shame from my past began to resurface itself through the grief of my infertility. I blamed my body for not conceiving and resented it for betraying me. I angrily mourned the way my womb bled month after month. I hung my head low and hid, not only the occurrence of but also the intense pain I felt surrounding my chemical pregnancy... my very early miscarriage. I kept my journey private fearing that if I spoke my story out loud I would jinx myself out of my miracle. I screamed into the abyss, praying that the goddess of hope would hear my cries. I cried loud and allowed my womb and throat to swim together in my own healing waters. And then—I shamed myself for doing so. I convinced myself that I was weak and therefore unworthy of becoming a mother. My once holy grief had become my demon of shame.

Shame is a demon of illusion. It strips us from our voice, our inner power, and our primal magic. To battle shame, we must be willing to face it and reclaim our power and truth. The journey is not easy, it requires us to become comfortable in our discomfort. It requires us to lean into our shame in the most intimate of ways.

Fast forward to March 2022, I held the most intimate ritual for myself right by the ocean. On this day, I felt my grief-mother call my shame forward, she asked me to allow each of my shameful thoughts to take up space in order to be fully witnessed. As I did this, I felt the waves of the ocean wash through me, almost as if they were cleansing me from the illusion that had covered my eyes. This cleansing act allowed me to lovingly see my journey in its totality. I saw my strength for walking through the grief of infertility for so long. I saw the tender way in which I picked myself up from the floor on that bloody morning when I lost my pregnancy. I witnessed the way in which Sean and I held one another through the brutality of this experience. I held the magic of knowing Luna. And then, with my hands placed lovingly on my womb, I began to dance and sing out loud. Breath by breath, I felt my shame unravel. Breath by breath, I felt myself surrender to the depth of my love.

There is bravery that exists when we allow ourselves to venture into the shadows of our pain. There is a magic that arises from the moment we choose to breathe into the crevices of our broken heart. We can hold our pain with the same reverence as we hold our hope and love. We are worthy of releasing our shame. All this time I thought Luna was bringing me home to her. And, perhaps, she was and, perhaps, she still is. But I think above all, Luna has been bringing me home to myself. She has been showing me that I am whole, that I am worthy, and that I am loved.

For that, I am forever grateful for being her mother.

ABOUT THE AUTHOR

ROXY SEWELL

Roxy Sewell, MS is a yogi, priestess, shadow worker, and word-witch. She is a healer who uses ritual and storytelling as her main source of magic. Roxy is dedicated to helping others to heal, to alchemize their grief and wounds, and to shed what no longer serves them so that they may unapologetically step forward into their sovereignty. She believes that we all have the power to become our own healers. Her most sacred work is done by sitting with clients, bearing witness to their journey, celebrating their rising, and holding space for all of who they are—both their shadow and their light. Roxy is the founder of Her Inner Labyrinth Healing, LLC and the creator of "An evening of myth and healing" a goddess-invoked and ritual-infused healing circle. Roxy lives in Atlanta, Georgia with her husband and their cat Neville.

Learn more and connect here:

https://www.instagram.com/roxy.sewell
roxy@herinnerlabyrinth.com

ABOUT THE PUBLISHER

SANCTUARY PUBLISHING

After getting fired from her first and last corporate job out of college, back in 2017, Annette Maria made a promise to herself and the Divine that she would live a life that is aligned with her soul. No longer trying to fit into the way others are telling her to be but to walk forward fearlessly carving her own path.

Part of that path is being a multi-passionate being that always thought it was wrong not to be able to choose just one thing to focus on. When Annette agreed to live a soul-led life, she made a vow to see her multi-passionate drive as a strength of being able to truly make anything happen. It unlocked a sense of play and child-like wonder in her journey.

That wonder took her on her own personal healing journey moving through abuse, sexual trauma, and anxiety/depression that ignited within her the fire to support others in their healing journey. Thus, she began a path of soul support for others, starting with yoga and meditation. Annette kept following the breadcrumbs that the Divine would offer her to take the next step forward. Alongside Sanctuary Publishing, she now supports individuals through Somatic Movement, Energy Healing, Shamanic Medicine, and Voice Activation to feel a sense of wholeness and presence to live a soul-led life themselves.

Sanctuary Publishing was one of those blessed breadcrumbs that was presented to her. Sanctuary Publishing was birthed out of a desire for our stories to be treated as sacred. Back in 2017, Annette received a channeled idea in the middle of an anxiety attack about a children's book called the Worry Wave. The Worry Wave is a beautiful story teaching children how to navigate their emotions and move through comparison. In her quest for getting published, she felt that her sacred story was just treated like another business transaction but didn't know where else to turn. Once the Worry Wave became published, Annette felt an urge to do things differently.

For those big dreams of being published to be truly celebrated and for the words written to be honored in a sacred birthing process. Sanctuary Publishing is here to do publishing with purpose. We highlight authors who are out in the world making a difference through their soul medicine to further reach the masses. They are the change makers, visionaries, and thought leaders that are rooted in bringing more love and peace to the planet.

Through multi-author books, solo-author books, and oracle/tarot card creation, we work with the mystical, spiritually driven leaders to bring their medicine even further out into the world.

If you resonate with Sanctuary Publishing and have a creation you wish to birth into the world, please email Annette Maria, hello@activationsbyannette.com. She will get back to you to feel into further alignment of working together.

Other ways to connect with Annette Maria through Sanctuary Publishing:

https://linktr.ee/sanctuarypublishing

Made in the USA
Las Vegas, NV
13 December 2023

82698107R00075